W9-BVI-816

Constructing Model Buildings

Constructing Model Buildings

John Cleaver

A Scopas Handbook

Academy Editions · London
St. Martins Press · New York

Scopas Handbooks

Series editor:
Christine Bernard

First published in Great Britain
in 1973 by Academy Editions
7 Holland Street London W8

First published in the U.S.A.
in 1973 by St. Martin's Press Inc.,
175 Fifth Avenue, New York N.Y. 10010
Affiliated publishers:
Macmillan Company Limited, London—
also at Bombay, Calcutta,
Madras and Melbourne—
The Macmillan Company
of Canada Limited, Toronto.

Library of Congress
catalog card number 73–79591

Printed and bound in Great Britain
at the Pitman Press, Bath

SBN hardback 85670 048 7
SBN paperback 85670 043 6

Frontispiece
An original design for a
multi-storeyed office block.
McCutchon Studio Ltd.

List of Contents

Chapter I

What kind of Model?

A model maker about to set out on the construction of a building model must decide at the outset to what use it will be put, for this decision affects the scale, material, durability, time and ultimate cost. Once the decision has been made it must be adhered to throughout the construction period right up to the finished product. Where a model has started off as a simple three-dimensional illustration of a design concept and then been used as a display model of the finished project, the alterations, additions and modifications will eventually become apparent and the model will lose all its freshness and evidence of a positive approach. The different types of building models can broadly be classified as those for:

1. Presentation to a Client

An architect or developer has to produce various draft schemes for consideration by his client. These schemes have to be sold not only to the client but in some cases to the future tenant or occupier, the bank or finance company backing the project, and the owners of the surrounding property. This type does not necessarily have to include landscaping, wall finishing, etc. A simple model of the building made in box form with the drawing elevations pasted on and coloured with water colours or poster colours serves to present a good impression of the proposed development in this case. Several such sketch schemes can be produced and offered for consideration.The acceptance of one at this stage of the proceedings can save considerable time and trouble when preparing a landscaped model for, say, the Local Authority's Planning Committee to consider.

The shapes should be kept as simple as possible, with no windows, doors or superimposed features. They should be made to a good quality finish and painted a uniform matt grey so that they can be handled and assembled in their correct relationship to each other. This assembly should be mounted on a matt black baseboard devoid of all landscaping, so that by viewing the model from all angles, it can be seen if the buildings and spaces between them form a pleasing harmony or not, before any detailed design is undertaken.

Such a model should be viewed in artificial light only if the direction of lighting can be controlled to simulate the direction of the sun. It is much better if the model is studied by placing it in its correct orientation relative to time of day in natural daylight conditions, making sure that it is not influenced by shadows cast by adjacent objects.

2. Planning Approval

A model is often used to support an application for development to the Local Authority, under the Town and Country Planning Acts, and is generally known as an 'environmental model'. Often a proposed development comes under severe criticism from a Planning Committee, not because the proposals are entirely out of keeping with their surroundings, but because the architect's drawings can only show the schemes in two dimensions, or at best a perspective sketch or 'impression'. Drawings tend to be in great detail, and the mass of information shown on a plan or elevation is rather forbidding to a lay-member of a committee or perhaps one who is concerned with the preservation of an old building. A model showing the proposed development in relation to the surrounding property which can be viewed from above and eye level, can swing the application to a favourable decision without the tedius processes of appealing against a refusal. It often happens that some fault in the development is brought out at this stage which can be corrected before planning application is actually made.

This type of model should be produced in natural colours wherever possible, with particular attention being paid to surrounding buildings so that in a borderline case the model can be taken to the site to confirm the mental picture built up in the minds of a planning committee.

3. Architectural Models

It is important that the model-maker should be capable of producing one to the requirements of an architect, if only to meet his request for a quick scheme.

The main difference between this and an environmental model is that it is usually constructed entirely from balsa wood, carefully jointed, and excluding all fine detail, so that the building volumes, planes and broad elevations can be studied before detailed design work is undertaken (see illus. 2). It is vital that sufficient balsa wood is purchased at the outset as the colour and grain of wood in one bundle can be completely unlike any other bundle, and this is most apparent when sections are joined at the edges to form a sheet.

2. Combined filling station and flats – broad planes and building masses

3. A long narrow building – front and rear are both in sharp focus

4. Models for Photography

There are instances when one may be called upon to produce a model which has to be photographed well in advance of a development being completed for inclusion in a brochure or catalogue. This would generally be a small scale model and there are many short cuts which can be used to speed up construction. For instance, if a building such as a school or office block is perfectly symmetrical it is only necessary to construct the model up to the half-way line. It is placed against a large mirror when photographed, thus giving an impression of a complete building. It is necessary to keep the distance from front to back as short as possible so that the whole model will be in focus when photographed (see illus. 3). Some distortion is allowable in this kind of model, the ground can be made to slope up slightly towards the rear, and a theatrical backcloth with clouds, etc., painted on can be included showing roads or rivers disappearing into the distance by following the laws of simple perspective. Alternatively a plain sky can be shown on the backcloth, clouds being added in the dark room by the use of a suitable cloud negative.

Chapter II

Tools and Materials

Tools

The model maker will require a few basic tools which he should get to know thoroughly, and he should practise with them on scrap material before setting out on the construction of an actual model. When assembling a tool kit, only buy the best items available. It is false economy to use cheap tools as they will not produce a good job and will have to be replaced frequently. Essential tools are:

1. A good knife with lots of spare blades, such as the Stanley knife, the sort with the retractable blade will be found to be the safest.
2. Engineers 'L' shaped tri-square, 4″ or 6″ is best. This is one of the most important tools as without its use it is impossible to cut at right angles. A plain edge is better than one marked off in inches or centimetres.
3. A steel ruler or straight-edge for cutting cardboard and plastic in conjunction with the Stanley knife.
4. Long-nosed pliers and combination pliers.
5. Tweezers – stamp collectors tweezers are quite useful for some jobs, but if a good pair of 8″ tweezers can be obtained these are much better.
6. A sharp, fine-toothed tenon saw with mitre-block for cutting mouldings and strip wood.
7. Scissors – the ordinary household type will do, but a visit to a Government surplus store or second-hand shop should produce a pair of surgical or hairdressers' scissors with long pointed blades. It is essential to keep these well sharpened and set as generally only the tips are used, most cutting operations being carried out with the Stanley knife.
8. Surgical scalpels are useful for the very fine cutting of balsa wood in architectural models, but extreme care is needed in their use. Unless it is the model maker's intention to construct balsa wood models principally, then a Stanley knife is quite adequate for the job. If scalpels are purchased these should be

of fine quality stainless steel, a good type has a steel handle with various shaped replaceable blades. These are quite cheap to obtain but should always be kept in a sponge-lined box when not in use, and extreme care must be used when fitting the blades to the handle.

9. Although not strictly a tool, a few hardwood blocks should be obtained, accurately constructed to form perfect right angles. Children's old-fashioned building bricks are ideal, as they are usually perfect cubes. They are used to hold corners of buildings into position whilst the glue is setting and can be used over and over again. Other similar blocks should be made accurately machined to form 15°, 30°, 45°, and 60° angled corners for the assembly of roof sections etc., and to use as gauges to check the consistency of building angles as the model takes shape.
10. Hand drills and a supply of high-speed steel drills up to $\frac{1}{4}''$ diameter.
11. Pin hammer, for driving in panel pins or steel dressmakers' pins and securing wooden mouldings in place.
12. Vice. A lightweight carpenter's vice is suitable, with a bench clamp so that it can be attached to a table in any suitable location.
13. Scriber. This is a sharp pointed skewer for accurate marking out on surfaces where a pencil cannot be used, or when scored lines are required such as brick courses, etc.
14. Scale rule. Used for taking off dimensions from architects' drawings. Three rules are usually required:

    No. 1 for site scales such as 1:1250, 1:2500, etc.

    No. 2 for normal architectural scales such as $\frac{1}{8}''$, $\frac{1}{4}''$, $\frac{3}{8}''$, $\frac{1}{2}''$, 1″ to 1′ 0″, and

    No. 3 for metric scales, i.e. 1:100, 1:50 etc.
15. Fret saw. This tool is used for sawing curved shapes such as contours in thin plywood or hardboard. It is not used on balsa wood or cardboard.
16. Files, Smooth and Second Cut engineers' files for trimming up the edges of polystyrene sheet, hardboard, perspex, plywood etc. Small 'watchmakers' files of various cross-

sections, i.e. square, triangular, flat, round, for finishing off holes cut into polystyrene sheet, and for the fine accurate filing of brass and copper tubes and wire etc.

17. Paint brushes. A good variety should be kept, of best quality. These include decorators' brushes ½″, 1″, 1½″. Artists' brushes, nylon bristle, up to ½″, and a few squirrel hair artists' brushes for fine lines and the painting of vehicles, figures etc.
18. Screwdrivers. Various sizes used mainly for attaching wooden cubes or blocks to baseboards.

N. B. The Chart on p. shows (by ref. to the above numbers) which tools are needed to make the component parts of the model.

Materials

The stock of materials will naturally be added to as time goes on, but at the outset it is suggested that a small stock of the following items is accumulated:

A. Good quality cardboard sheets. These are sold by art shops under various names such as 'Bristol Board', 'Mounting Board', 'Fashion-plate board' etc. Probably the best one to start with is 'Fashion-plate board' and in fact most references in this book are to this material. It is still very much a matter of choice as to which grade or type is used as the model progresses.

B. Balsa wood in sheets and blocks. This should always be purchased in a quantity to make sure that there is sufficient to finish the model in hand, as small bits added at a later date will never match up (see appendix Bi).

C. Polystyrene sheet in two or three thicknesses, 0·052″, 0·020″, 0·040″. The type with a dull or matt surface on one side is best for painting purposes (see appendix Bii).

D. Expanded polystyrene sheet or blocks. This is a super-lightweight material sold generally in square tiles for fixing to ceilings for insulation and decorative purposes. It is also available in block form and is used extensively in modern packaging to protect photographic and other apparatus in transit.

E. Plexiglas or perspex sheets $\frac{1}{32}$ thick (0·79 mm) for windows, etc. (see appendix Biii).

F. Chipboard $\frac{1}{2}''$ or $\frac{5}{8}''$ thick in sheet sizes as and when required for bases.

G. Enamel paint is sold by model railway shops in very small tins, and is obtainable in gloss or matt finishes in an amazing variety of colours. It is also possible to obtain these paints in metallic finishes and in aerosol cans for spraying, from your local toy shop.

H. Adhesives.

(i) Clear Bostik all-purpose adhesive which will stick most materials. If any plastic items are to be fixed together it is best to experiment on a scrap piece before applying it to the model itself as there might be an unfavourable reaction.

(ii) Tube glue. Sold under various trade names. This is an adhesive generally for sticking wood and cardboard and should not be used on plastics.

(iii) Polystyrene cement. As the name implies, this is a special cement for polystyrene sheet and rod only. It should be used sparingly and as it is very 'liquid' great care must be taken not to allow any to drop onto the surface of the polystyrene sheet where it is not wanted, otherwise it is liable to dissolve the polystyrene sheet locally, causing disfigurement.

(iv) Balsa cement. Another special cement used on balsa wood only. This is sold in small tubes so that it can be accurately placed on the section to be joined. Clear Bostik can also be used to join balsa wood together, however.

(v) Expanded polystyrene cement. Sold in large tubes or tins, generally for the fixing of expanded polystyrene ceiling tiles and it should only be used on this material.

(vi) Office paste, sold under various trade names. Used for attaching paper to cardboard, and in other places where paper has to be attached to a base material.

(vii) Sellotape clear tape. Obtainable in rolls of various widths. Used for holding sections of a model together whilst the glue or adhesive is setting. It is also used for masking out areas on Plexiglass or perspex which do not have to be painted.

I. Hardwood mouldings. A selection of these should be kept to hand in various small sections such as rectangular, quadrant, right angle and round dowel rod of various diameters.

J. Plaster of paris, the fine, known as 'Dental Plaster', is best. Do not keep too much in stock as it goes stale after a short time.

N.B. See charts on p. 16 and 17 which describes the tools and materials needed for the component parts of the model.

Component parts of models and the tools necessary to produce them.

Tool No. on list	1. Stanley knife	2. Tri-square	3. Steel straight-edge	4. Pliers, various	5. Tweezers	6. Tenon saw	7. Scissors	8. Scapels	9. Guide blocks	10. Hand drill	11. Pin hammer	12. Vice	13. Scriber	14. Scale rules	15. Fret saw	16. Files	17. Paint brushes	18. Screwdrivers
Baseboard (contoured)	x	x	x			x				x	x		x	x	x		x	x
Baseboard (flat)		x	x			x				x	x		x	x			x	x
Bungalow	x	x	x	x	x		x	x	x	x		x	x	x		x	x	
Bush	x			x	x		x							x			x	
Canopy (garage)	x	x	x		x					x			x	x		x	x	
Car wash	x	x	x	x	x	x	x		x	x	x	x	x	x		x	x	
Carpet	x		x		x		x							x				
Chimney	x	x	x		x			x	x	x	x		x	x			x	
Curtains	x		x		x		x							x				
Door, folding	x	x	x		x		x						x	x			x	
Door, roller	x	x	x		x		x						x	x			x	
Door, personnel	x	x	x		x			x						x			x	
Fence, chainlink	x		x		x									x		x		
Fence, slatted	x	x	x		x								x	x		x		
Grass																	x	
Grill flooring	x		x											x				
Hedge							x										x	
House	x	x	x		x		x	x	x			x	x	x		x	x	
Kiosk	x	x	x		x		x	x	x			x	x	x		x	x	
Lake	x		x											x	x	x	x	
Lift shaft		x	x			x		x	x		x			x			x	x
Pavement	x	x	x				x	x					x	x			x	
Petrol, brand sign	x				x		x							x		x	x	
Petrol pump	x	x	x		x			x		x				x		x	x	
River	x		x											x	x	x	x	
Roof (flat)	x	x	x					x	x					x			x	
Roof (pitched)	x	x	x		x		x	x	x				x	x			x	
Shop	x	x	x		x		x	x	x	x		x	x	x		x	x	
Stick light	x			x	x									x		x	x	
Street lamp	x			x	x									x		x	x	
Swimming pool	x		x											x	x	x	x	
Tree, deciduous				x	x		x							x			x	
Tree, evergreen				x	x		x							x			x	
Tree, ornamental				x	x									x			x	
Ventilator	x	x	x		x			x					x	x		x	x	
Window	x	x	x		x		x	x		x			x	x		x	x	

Component parts of models and materials necessary to produce them.

	Acrylic sheet (plexiglas)	Ball pen refills	Balsa wood	Bandages	Cardboard	Chipboard	Cork chippings	Dowel rod	Flock paper	Flock powder	Foam rubber	Glass fibre	Hardboard	Letraset transfer letters	Loofa	Paint	Patterned paper	Pipe cleaners	Plaster-of-paris	Plywood	Polystyrene sheet	Sponge	Stripwood mouldings	Welding rod wire	Wet and dry emery paper	Wire, various gauges
Baseboard (contoured)			x	x	x	x	x	x				x	x			x			x	x			x			
Baseboard (flat)					x	x										x							x			
Bungalow	x		x		x			x								x	x				x		x	x		
Bush											x				x	x						x				x
Canopy (garage)	x		x		x			x					x	x		x					x			x	x	
Car wash	x		x		x			x								x	x	x			x		x	x		
Carpet									x																	
Chimney			x		x			x								x	x				x					
Curtains									x																	
Door, folding			x		x											x					x					
Door, roller			x		x			x								x					x					
Door, personnel	x		x		x											x					x					
Fence, chainlink	x													x												
Fence, slatted			x																		x		x			
Grass									x	x																
Grill flooring	x													x												
Hedge											x				x							x				
House	x		x		x			x								x	x				x			x		
Kiosk	x		x		x											x	x				x			x	x	
Lake	x															x										
Lift shaft			x																		x		x			
Pavement			x		x											x	x									
Petrol, brand sign					x			x								x								x		
Petrol pump	x		x		x											x					x					
River	x															x										
Roof (flat)			x		x																x				x	
Roof (pitched)			x		x												x				x					
Shop	x		x		x			x						x		x	x				x			x		
Stick light		x														x								x		x
Street lamp		x														x								x		x
Swimming pool	x															x										
Tree, deciduous											x					x						x				x
Tree, evergreen																x						x				x
Tree, ornamental							x				x					x						x				x
Ventilator			x		x			x								x							x			
Window	x															x										

Chapter III

Four Basic Techniques

Having obtained the basic requirements the model-maker must practise with them so that when a particular model is to be made, he will select the tool and method necessary at every stage of construction. This will leave his mind clear to work out details of the model as it progresses without being troubled by problems in construction. Four basic methods are described here; the number or letter in brackets refers to the item on the Tool or Material List on pp 16 and 17.

Method 1

Material:	Cardboard (A).
Tools:	Stanley knife (1), Tri-square (3), Straight-edge (2).
Problem:	To produce a straight clean accurate cut.

The piece of cardboard should be placed on a flat firm surface on a larger section of scrap cardboard. The line to be cut is marked with a 3H or 4H pencil sharpened to a 'chisel' point to give a thin firm line. After marking the cardboard with a pencil line, the straight-edge (2) should be placed against the line and held in place by spreading the thumb and finger along it, making double sure that the fingers do not protrude beyond the edge of the ruler. The card to be cut will already have been placed on a sheet of scrap cardboard on a firm working surface. The model maker should be so placed that he is looking directly down onto the pencil line and can see it for its entire length. The Stanley knife (1) with a good blade is drawn lightly at first along the pencil line up against the straight-edge, followed by a firmer cut. It might take several strokes of the knife to cut through if it is thick cardboard, but provided the Stanley knife is kept perfectly upright at all times and not allowed to waver, the result will be a good clean cut.

If a line has to be drawn and cut at right angles to the edge produced by cutting along the straight-edge, then the tri-square (3) is placed against the line and held firmly whilst the Stanley knife is drawn along the long arm of the tri-square thus producing a cut at right angles to the previous one.

When window apertures or other square sections have to be cut out, it is necessary to put the point of the Stanley knife firmly through the cardboard, and cut *away* from each corner. If an attempt is made to cut *into* a corner, invariably the slope of the knife blade continues the cut into the section of 'wall' beyond the window leaving an untidy appearance to the finished model.

Method 2

Material: Balsa wood (B), adhesive H.iv.
Tools: Scalpels (8), Straight-edge (3), Tri-square (2). Wooden block (9).
Problem: Cutting, assembling and joining balsa wood.

Balsa wood is a very lightweight material with a natural tendency to split along the grain. All cuts should be made first *across* the grain with a scalpel (8) held steady against the straight-edge (3) or tri-square (2), extending beyond the final length of the line into the scrap wood beyond. When the cuts across the grain are completed the cuts *along* the grain can be made to join them up, but these should be made carefully to avoid splitting. When making architectural models where a very tidy corner is required on a model building, the scalpel should be held at an angle of about 45° rather than vertical so that when the pieces are joined together with balsa wood cement (H.iv) they will form a very neat join. Remember that the pencil line must be drawn to the *inside* dimension of the building, allowing for the thickness of the balsa wood to take care of the wall thickness. When assembling two pieces of balsa wood to form a right-angled wall in this way, use is made of a wooden block (9) whilst the adhesive is setting to make sure of a correct right angle.

Balsa wood is normally purchased in strips 3′ 0″ long and about 3″ wide, but some $\frac{1}{4}$″ and $\frac{1}{2}$″ wide strips of $\frac{1}{8}$″ thick balsa wood should also be obtained for edging (see appendix B.i). The 3″ wide strips as purchased are not wide enough for use directly on the model, so it is necessary to join two or more pieces edge to edge to give sheets of balsa wood 6″ or 9″ wide. The method of joining along the relatively thin edges is to first place a sheet of thin tissue paper flat on the working surface. If ordinary tissue paper is not available a good substitute is paper handkerchief tissue – this is only to prevent excess cement from attaching the balsa wood to the table! A good film of balsa wood cement is squeezed along the edges of the sections to be joined, and these are then placed together and put flat on the table making sure that the entire length of join is lying on tissue paper. More tissue paper is then placed on top and a suitable weight such as a heavy book is placed on top until the adhesive is set. After the appropriate drying time the book and top tissue can be removed and the sheet of balsa wood checked to see that it is joined properly. If everything is in order, any tissue adhering to the balsa wood can be removed by very gently sanding off with a sheet of super-fine sandpaper wrapped around a block of wood, following the grain of the balsa wood.

Method 3

Material:	Polystyrene sheet (C), adhesive H.iii.
Tools:	Stanley knife (1), Tri-square (2), Straight-edge (3).
Problem:	Cutting, joining and forming polystyrene sheet.

Polystyrene sheet is a versatile material having many uses in model making, but needs to be handled and used carefully for best results. It should preferably be stored flat, and kept free from dust and grit (see appendix B.ii).

Setting out can be done with a pencil. To obtain an improved surface for drawing, rub material gently with a fine abrasive such as whiting or french chalk.

Polystyrene sheet can be scored and snapped easily, it can be cut with a knife, sawn and planed. If a slightly raised edge remains after cutting, this can be removed with a fine sandpaper block. When joining sheets or strips together butt joints are usually employed and are most satisfactory, 'proud' surfaces at joints being rubbed away with a fine sandpaper block. *Cement should always be applied sparingly and spread as evenly as possible.* Blobs and accumulations of excess cement can result in distorted surfaces due to prolonged chemical action on the material.

When painting, surfaces should be free from dust and grease. Two thin coats of paint will produce a better finish than one thick coat.

Method 4

Material:	Plexiglas or perspex (E).
Tools	Stanley knife (1), Tri-square (2), Straight-edge (3), Pliers (4).
Problem:	Cutting Plexiglas sheet.

This material is usually supplied with a protective paper covering on both sides which should be left in place until the last possible moment, to protect the Plexiglas from scratching (see Appendix B.iii). The size of the required section is marked in pencil on the protective covering and then the material is scored using the Stanley knife (1), tri-square (2) and straight-edge (3). The sheet of Plexiglas is treated as in window glass cutting, by placing it over the edge of the table or bench and then firmly bearing down on the protruding portion so that it breaks along the line. If a square has to be cut out of the corner of a large sheet, it is preferable to drill a very small hole at the intersection of the marked lines, otherwise the whole sheet might split when the section is being broken away. When cutting thinner pieces of Plexiglas, it is sometimes easier to progressively bend the two pieces apart with the thumbs and forefingers of each hand, starting from the outside of the sheet. Small strips are broken away from the main sheet after scoring by carefully breaking them away with pliers (4).

The same procedures apply when using thick perspex sheeting, but with the thick material it is necessary to score the lines from both sides before snapping off.

Hints and Tips

One main object in making model buildings, whether architectural or environmental, is to form an idea as quickly as possible how the finished project will look. This does not necessarily mean that the actual stages of construction can be rushed along, but the following hints and tips will prove useful in the construction of the model:

1. Have patience!
2. Always 'think out' the model before obtaining any materials.
3. Limit the variety of materials you use for the main buildings – i.e. do not start off with cardboard houses, then switch to polystyrene and balsa wood.

4. Work out the construction stages, making a few notes if necessary so that you do not, for instance, have to cut holes in the baseboard after buildings are in place.
5. Ask yourself 'What is the model to illustrate?' then answer truthfully if a smaller scale model would suffice thus saving on time, cost and space.
6. Never use a material heavier than it needs to be. It is better to use a light material properly braced, rather than an out-of-scale thick material.
7. Never use wet materials such as plaster of paris when a dry material can be used.
8. *Always* use a tri-square to cut out cardboard, etc., at right angles. A guess is never accurate and causes trouble as the model takes shape.
9. Make sure that any items to be glued on or painted are ready *before* they are required for fitting in place.
10. If the adhesive or paint used recommends 2–4 hours drying time, then make sure that this time is allowed for so that the sections are not disturbed whilst drying.
11. When holding fragile buildings or structures in a vice for sticking always use sponge rubber on the vice jaws to prevent over tightening of the vice.
12. Never apply paint to a model if you intend to sandpaper or file any other item before the paint has properly dried – the dust can never be removed.
13. Keep Stanley knife blades and scalpels *sharp*, discard them when they get blunt.
14. Always keep a piece of fresh cardboard on the bench top when cutting out so that the tip of the knife blade does not follow an old cut, thus spoiling the piece being cut out.
15. Use plenty of dressmakers' steel pins to hold bits and pieces in place while the glue sets.
16. When using brick and tile patterned papers make sure that the brick courses line up when a butt joint has to be made in the paper.
17. When assembling several buildings on a baseboard, try to work from the centre of the board towards the outside so that

you do not catch the perimeter buildings with your sleeves, etc.

18. Always cover the model at the end of each working session with a plastic sheet to prevent dust settling.
19. Never try to mix and match paint colours in bad light, or artificial light if the original paint has been mixed in daylight.
20. Always attach every component part of a model firmly. The natural tendency is for people to 'see if the little cars are stuck down'.
21. To repeat the prime rule: *Have patience!*

Chapter IV

Preparing the Project

Scaling

We are now about to set out on the construction of a model of a development project, and the first thing to decide on is the scale. The smallest scale we can make a model so that it doesn't look like a coloured map is 1 to 1250. At this scale individual buildings and roads will be identified as will be seen from a study of an Ordnance Survey map to this scale. Average size houses will appear as $\frac{1}{8}''$ cubes, but factories and public halls will be up to 1″ in length, and as such can be constructed in some detail. The value of this scale is that on a baseboard 2′ 0″ square there can be shown a large enough area of countryside to identify a particular building site in relation to its environment, and by judicious use of scaled contours its height relative to the surrounding countryside can be judged. It should be pointed out at this stage that it is important to exaggerate the vertical scale by at least three times, otherwise a great deal of careful work only succeeds in producing a model with slight changes in height, and apparent realism is lost. The method of construction for this type of contoured model is explained in detail in the section dealing with baseboards on p. 33.

4. Small scale model (1:1250) which covers a large area of territory, but includes quite a lot of detail

As the scale of the model is increased to 1 to 500, more detail is possible, and a model of a housing project for instance can be made with individual trees becoming recognisable, traffic and figures appearing in the streets, and roads, rivers, etc., looking quite authentic. So far, all scales mentioned deal with sections of the countryside generally in order to locate a particular site in its surroundings. The main purpose of this sort of model is to be able to show to a client or committee that the proposed development is in keeping with its surroundings, in particular when the 'Green Belt' is under discussion.

The best scale to work to in order to produce a model in reasonable detail is 1 to 200. This approximates to 1″ to 16′ 0″ and a model on this scale is usually small enough to be moved around, but at the same time large enough to give a very good idea of the proposed development. It must be borne in mind that once a model is larger than 1 to 100 or 1″ to 8′ 0″ then considerable detail will be called for which generally involves far more work than is really necessary in order to illustrate a particular site although simple architect's models of building sections may exceed this scale at times.

One factor to be considered in favour of a 1″ to 8′ 0″ or 1 to 100 model is that many items produced for 00 scale model railways can be included. This scale is 4 mm to 1′ 0″, which is quite close to 1 to 100, and by careful use of printed brick and tile papers for instance, a quick model can be produced to illustrate a scheme without any pretence to absolute accuracy of scale in brick courses, etc., It must be emphasised however that brick and tile papers of this type can only be included in relatively small areas, as the smoothness of them does not look natural in large pieces.

If the project in hand is a development involving say several blocks of flats, then it is probably best to construct a site model showing the flats and garages, etc., in their correct positions with the surrounding property included for comparison, and a model to a scale of 1 to 50 or 1″ to 4′ 0″ showing a layout of one complete floor with the individual rooms clearly defined. This would be able to show such detail as sink units, cookers, serving hatches, doors, radiators, and other similar items. It is also possible at this stage to produce furniture to the same scale so that a potential purchaser can see not only the arrangement of rooms and passageways, but would also obtain a good idea of how individual items of furniture fit into the rooms. A few figures can be included to give a good idea of size, and this is of use to the estate agent responsible for selling or leasing the property, after the architect or developer has finished the construction.

Any scale larger than 1″ to 4′ 0″ or 1 to 50, (such as 1″ to 1′ 0″), is generally outside the scope of a building model due to its size and construction, but sometimes it is necessary to construct a model to this scale to illustrate an arrangement of furniture for instance in a restaurant.

Six Vital Steps

The next vital step is to gather together all information necessary to carry out construction as, once the model starts to take shape it is very disturbing to find that some feature has to be modified or remade due to lack of research before construction began. The first and most important item is an **architect's drawing of the plan** and all elevations of the proposed development. This must be to the same scale as the proposed model so that direct measurements can be taken from a print, otherwise continuity of construction is lost when measurements have to be taken and then converted to another scale. The second item of importance is an **Ordnance Survey map** of the locality to as large a scale as possible, showing contours and levels around the development site. Armed with this map it is now necessary to **visit the site** to check that no new buildings have been erected since the map was prepared. It is also suggested that **photographs are taken** of all buildings and features which will appear on the model, from all sides. A good idea is to arrange for a car or other object of known dimensions to be parked against a building before photographing it, so that when the prints are developed (8″ × 10″ are the best size), it is a simple matter to divide the height of the car into the height of the building and thus arrive at the height of the building itself. Instead of black and white prints it is sometimes better to take colour transparencies of the various items so that a colour reference is to hand when finishing off the model. The drawback of course is that when they are screened one cannot make notes about the dimensions. Possibly the best idea is to take detailed photographs in black and white, with a few colour transparencies just for colour reference. **A particular note** must be made of trees (size, colouring and type), as these items, if not reproduced properly, can completely alter the concept of a model. Incidentally, it is always necessary to consider models as being depicted in summer with trees and grass in a suitable green colour.

All photographs can then be **mounted in a loose-leaf binder** together with sketches, maps, notes, material references such as brick manufacturers' brochures, and any other related paperwork. Once construction is under way no time needs to be lost trying to find a note among the accumulated glue, cardboard, wire, sponge, balsa wood and other items.

Devote a special room, or corner of a room, to the model-making area, so that a good bench or table is always available. This must be rigid and of a convenient height for sitting at. There must be good lighting available, as it is not always possible to ensure a good daylight location. In any case, if you do depend too much on daylight then this naturally restricts the time when you can make your models. Make sure you have a cupboard or shelving to store all the pieces of cardboard, balsa wood, plastic sheeting, perspex, wire, etc.

Chapter V

The Baseboard

We are now ready to start work on the first essential, namely the baseboard. This will vary according to whether you plan to work on a flat, sloping, or contoured site.

5. Typical small filling station on a flat site

The Flat Site

The best material for constructing the base for a flat site model is chipboard. This is a man-made material constructed from wood chippings bonded together under pressure, and is usually produced in 8′ 0″ × 4′ 0″sheets. Most do-it-yourself shops or timber yards sell it in cut sizes, and in practice it will be found that 24″ × 24″ or even 20″ × 20″ will be big enough for the majority of models constructed to a scale of 1 to 200 or $\frac{1}{16}$″ × 1′ 0″. The best approach is to decide on the size required for your base and then get it cut accurately to size making sure that all corners are right angles as the sides will be used for measuring dimensions. Chipboard is available in several thicknesses but for the purpose of model making $\frac{1}{2}$″ is usually suitable. If $\frac{5}{8}$″ or $\frac{3}{4}$″ is used then the model becomes too heavy to

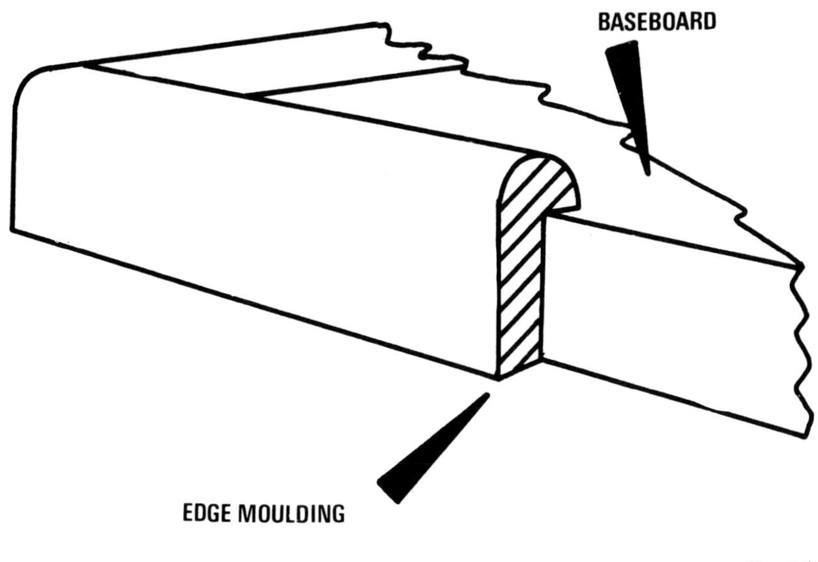

Figure 1

move around easily and damage can result. The edges of chipboard are always rough where they have been cut, and if left in this state they will disintegrate and the model will suffer damage as a result. It is necessary therefore to construct a hardwood frame around the baseboard. We shall need some special moulding for this which is obtainable from most timber yards under the description of 'hockey stick'. This peculiar description arises from the fact that when looked at in cross-section it vaguely resembles a hockey stick (see fig. 1).

Using the mitre block and fine-toothed tenon saw it is necessary to cut the moulding accurately at 45° on the corners to enclose the baseboard, assuming the baseboard is square or rectangular in shape. There are instances where a site is flat and level but where a basement to a block of flats for example is necessary. In this case it is a good idea to use an edging strip as shown, deep enough to take up the difference in levels (see fig. 2). This idea can be used in several cases where an excavation had to be indicated on a model such as deep gravel pits or lakes. The next operation is to give the baseboard two coats of white hardboard primer or emulsion paint, lightly sanded down between coats. This gives a good surface for laying out the buildings, roadways, etc. Assuming we are working to a scale of 1 to 200 or $\frac{1}{16}'' = 1'\ 0''$ then we shall have a drawing to this scale available.

We place the drawing on the baseboard with carbon paper between the drawing and the baseboard and with a hard pencil and straight-edge go over the main lines of buildings and other features.

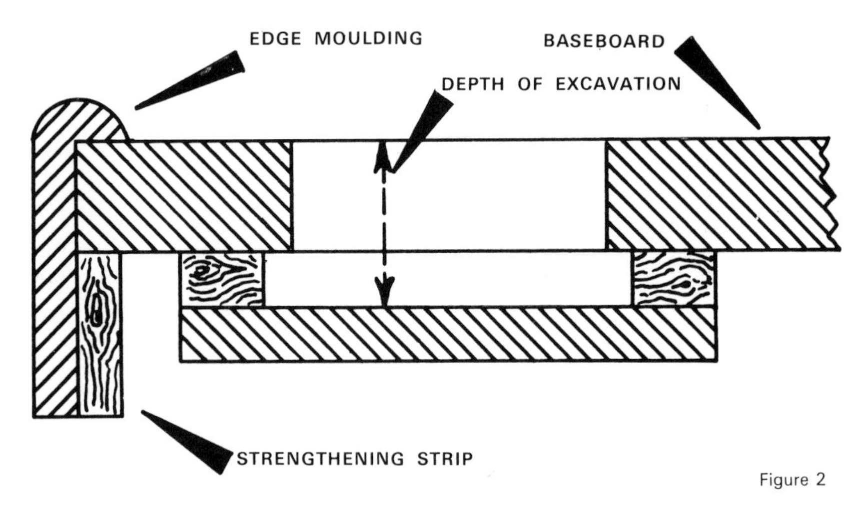

Figure 2

Another way to take off the main dimensions without the use of carbon paper is to prick through the drawing at various important points with a sharp pointed tool, and join up the points on the baseboard with pencil and straight-edge. The baseboard at this stage of the proceedings will be a simple duplication of the drawing which was prepared previously, and the baseboard level can then generally be regarded as the road level on the actual site. Obviously there will be pavements to the roads so taking a suitable piece of cardboard we trace off with the carbon paper all pavements, making due allowance for traffic cross-overs which have to be marked and then cut at an angle with the Stanley knife blade to represent the ramp down to the road surface (see fig. 3). With good quality cardboard this is not a difficult operation, but if cheap cardboard is used it is impossible to produce a clean edge. The pavement sections are cut out using the tip of the Stanley knife and a firm even pressure. The sections of pavement are next firmly glued to the baseboard using clear Bostik or similar adhesive. Using our carbon paper we next produce card sections to the size of the buildings which will eventually occupy various locations on the model, these pieces are attached *temporarily* to their sites by panel pins or drawing pins (see fig. 4). The necessity for attaching them temporarily is so that when the ground is painted on the

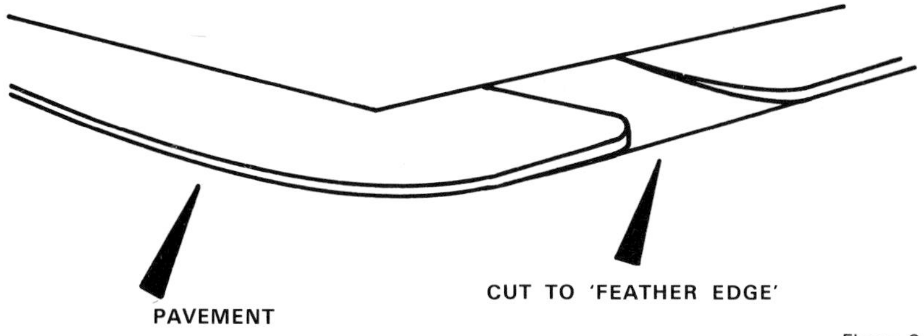

Figure 3

model, the building bases can be lifted for incorporation into the building models still to be made, leaving a clear spot for registering their size onto the base. In some instances the buildings will not in fact be attached to their bases, but alternative designs of buildings may be produced to obtain an effect of different designs on a particular site.

We have now reached a stage in construction where we have the baseboard marked out with the position of all buildings, and the pavements have been placed in their correct location. In the case of environmental models we next have to prepare the ground areas between the buildings for decorating in natural colours. If there are cases where a grassed area for instance is raised up above its surroundings, then this section is cut out of cardboard and glued into place. Sometimes a particular feature such as a mound has to be shown, this can be modelled out of plaster of paris, or one of the patent powder fillers sold at decorators' shops for stopping up cracks in walls. We then obtain a supply of tube paints known as Cryla colours. It is suggested that the serious model maker obtain the special booklet on the material from an artists' materials supplier and experiments with thin and thick applications to get the feel of it.

Using our Cryla colours we now paint all areas of the baseboard we have constructed so far, thinning down the paint with water or 'Cryla medium' for roads and pavements, but applying it thicker for gardens and fields. We can give it a stippled effect to simulate grass on small scale models, and if several shades of green are mixed on the pallet, with a little yellow on the side, using the tip of a large flat artists' brush from one colour to the other, a very natural appearance of field grass can be obtained, with 'buttercup areas' where needed. A change of green can be applied around entrances to a field or where footpaths occur so that movement of people or cattle can be indicated by implication, thus giving the model a certain amount of 'life' and getting away from the somewhat mechanical interpretation of a set of architectural drawings.

If gardens and landscaping come into the model, then thicker blobs of colour represent clumps of flowers or even cabbages. A few touches of vermillion red or yellow gives a very good impression of flowers and does a great deal towards giving the model a natural look. At this stage it is not necessary to complete the landscaping altogether, but it *is* important to get the main areas complete, especially where trees and hedges will be created, as, once items start to rise above the level of the baseboard it becomes more difficult to pass a paint brush between the obstacles.

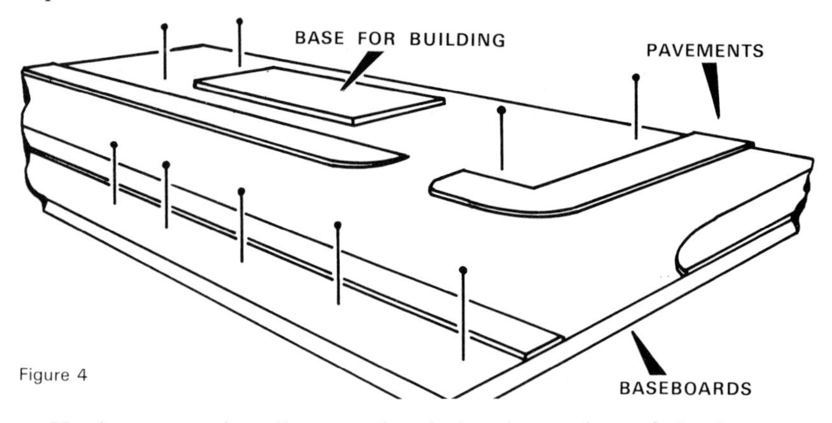

Figure 4

Having now virtually completed the decoration of the base, we have to mark off the position of trees, poles, etc.: measure the distance on the plan from the edges'. To simplify matters, it is not necessary to use a ruler, but a straight strip of white card 1″ wide will suffice. Each tree or pole on the plan is marked off in turn along the edge of the card its distance from the border and this in turn is transferred to the baseboard. Using the point of a scriber make a mark on the baseboard and then taking the wheel-brace with a $\frac{1}{16}$″ diameter drill, drill a hole for approximately half the depth of the baseboard, and then insert a match or cocktail stick to mark the location (see fig. 4). At a much later stage of the model, in fact when all the buildings are in place, we shall be replacing these sticks with the proper trees or poles. Using sticks in this manner cross check their distance from each other, and their correct distance from the buildings, to check for errors that may have been made earlier.

Sloping and Contoured Sites

A very quick and cheap method of producing contours on a 'sketch model' is to use expanded polystyrene ceiling tiles or sheets. These are generally $\frac{3}{16}''$ or $\frac{1}{4}''$ thick, at a scale of $\frac{1}{8}'' = 1'\ 0''$, therefore the changes in level occur every 1′ 6″ to 2′ 0″ in height on the actual site, which is quite acceptable. The expanded polystyrene should be cut

6. Apartment block and petrol-filling station on a sloping site. Scale 1:200

cleanly with a very sharp knife or blade, and after assembly with the correct tile adhesive can be rounded off or even 'sculptured' with a hot soldering iron. It is a fascinating material to work with and has the benefits of being both cheap and light. Several experiments should be done before starting on a model.

If a more accurate or permanent model is to be produced, and time is not so important, then a different method of construction is called for. Another method would be by using the drawing to establish the lowest point of the site, and using this as a datum mark off all other points as heights above this marker. If a model is to be constructed to a 1 to 200 scale or 1 to 100 scale, it will generally be about 24″ square, so it is necessary to establish check points for heights above the lowest point at a spacing of about 2″–3″ between points. In particular the position and size of all buildings with their relative height above the base point must be firmly established, and plywood or hardboard sections slightly larger than the buildings must then be cut out. Having decided by how much the slope is to be emphasised, we cut spacing blocks of wood (see fig. 5) corresponding to the height of the building or tree base above the baseboard.

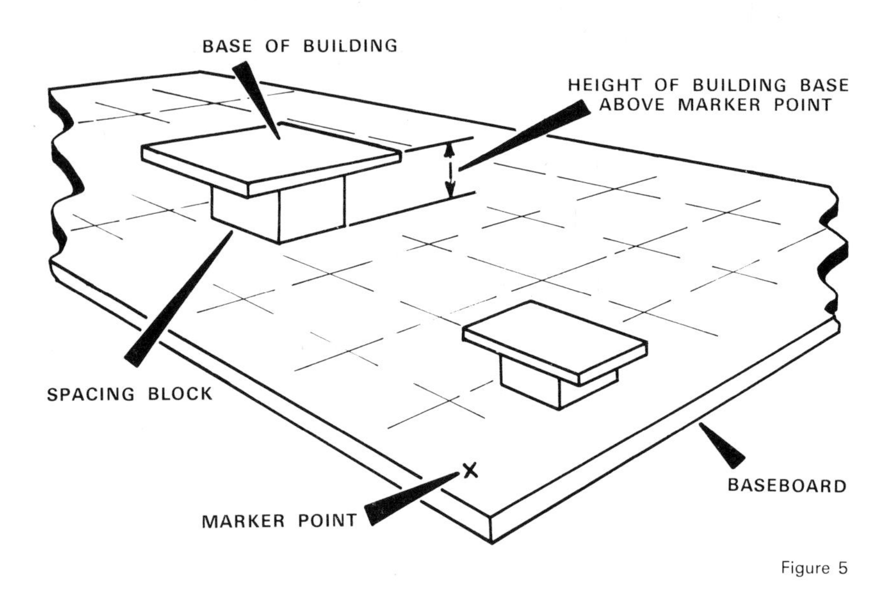

Figure 5

The next step is to cut a series of $\frac{1}{4}''$ diameter dowel pegs corresponding in length to the various check points on the plan (i.e. their height above the marker point) plus half the thickness of the chipboard base. As an example, if a $\frac{1}{2}''$ thick baseboard is being used, then each dowel must be equal to the height of the check point above the base, plus $\frac{1}{4}''$.

Having marked out the baseboard with the location of the height check points, we now drill it on the centres of all the check points half way through, then taking the dowel piece apply glue to the end of it and lightly tap it into place on the baseboard. The stage is now reached where we have a 'porcupine' effect, with the baseboard covered in pegs or dowels, with building and tree bases (see fig. 6).

We shall need filling material as light in weight as possible, rolls of fibre glass normally sold for insulating house lofts is ideal, it should be handled with rubber gloves, as sometimes an irritation can be set up on the skin by the tiny fibres. It is now possible to break off sections of the fibre glass material and place them in position between and around the pegs and wooden sections fixed to the base. Continue to add pieces of fibre glass until they are fairly firmly packed in, and only $\frac{1}{4}''$ or so of the dowels are protruding. The material will feel reasonably 'springy' to the touch between the dowels. Now obtain a section of wire-netting with small mesh, such as 'chicken wire'. It may be necessary to cut this in various places in order to thread it over the building bases, but make as few cuts as possible to give greater stability. Placing this over the fibre glass make sure that the dowel pegs still protrude $\frac{1}{4}''$ or so, and attach the wire-netting to the fibre glass with hair-pins or thin wire staples, and to the dowels with thin fuse wire or adhesive tape. Some cut lengths of bandage should be threaded through the mesh in a few places, 'finger bandage' 1″ wide is ideal.

Now the packing must be fixed within the confines of the baseboard; so you will need some lengths of $\frac{1}{4}''$ plywood or hardboard as long as the baseboard sides, and $\frac{1}{4}''$ higher than the highest point, measured from the *underside* of the baseboard. These are put into place to form a 'box' with the model baseboard as its base, and the profile of the wire-netting position marked on them. A line is then marked $\frac{1}{4}''$ above this line and using a fretsaw the shape is cut out. The side pieces can then be glued and pinned to the baseboard, thus giving an overall picture of how the ground will finally look (see fig. 7).

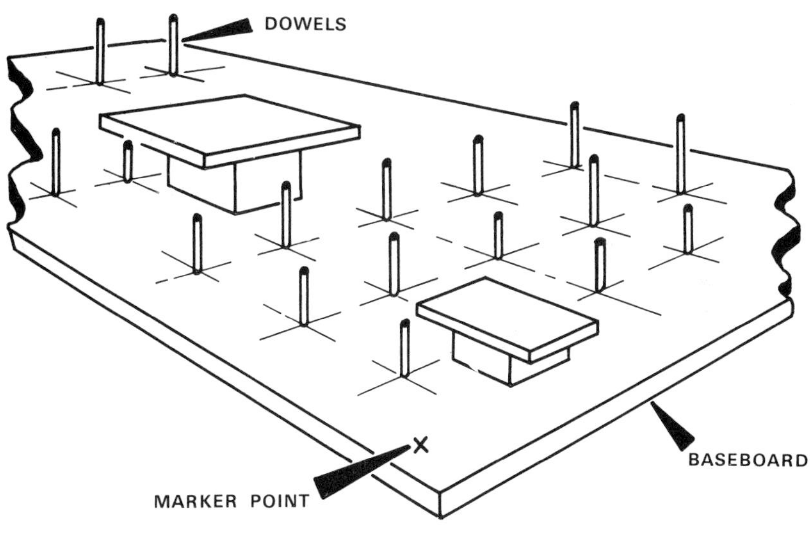

Figure 6

Pieces of 2″–3″ wide bandages should now be dipped in a thin mixture of plaster of paris, and placed on the wire-netting mesh in alternating directions, first brushing over the interwoven bandage pieces with plaster of paris mixture to give a key. Continue to laminate the bandage sections until they reach the height of the dowel

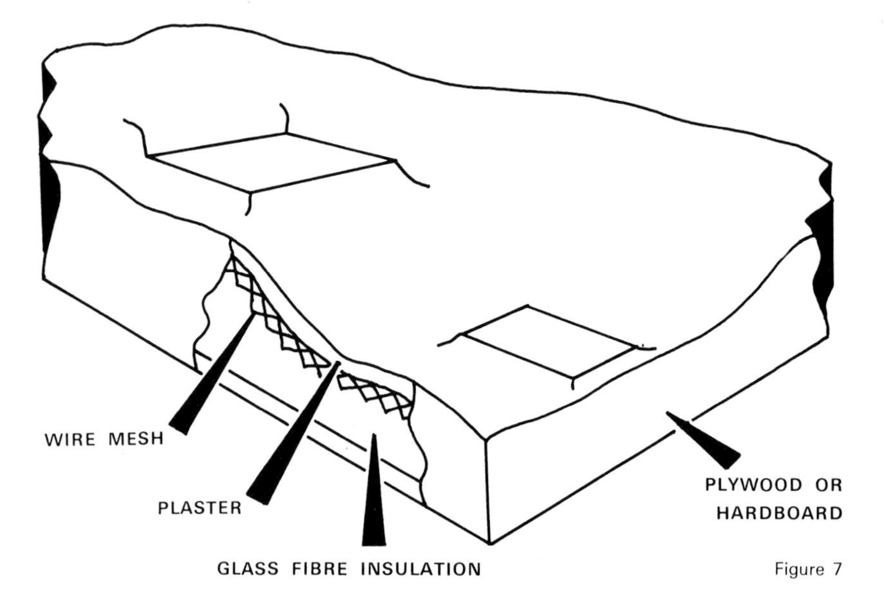

Figure 7

pegs and building bases, by this time the model should start to feel hard to the touch and give quite a solid sound when knocked.

The final basic operation is to mix some thicker plaster of paris and spread this entirely over the model, like icing a cake using a spatula or small trowel. The plaster of paris should bring the ground level up to the shapes cut into the side pieces round the baseboard (see fig. 7).

The model at this stage of construction should be put aside in a warm (*not hot*) room for the plaster to gradually dry out for at least three days so that drying out can be a gradual process. A warm damp cloth should be wiped over the surface after twenty-four hours, and again when the model is ready to be worked on again. After three days or longer, spray the plaster surfaces with an aerosol primer or sealer. This will give a good non-porous surface for painting on and helps to give better 'control' to the colours. Using Cryla colours paint on the various areas of open ground, grassed areas, building areas, roads and pavements, etc. Any retaining walls for banks which are necessary should be constructed from card or plywood and be securely pinned or glued in position before the plaster of paris is applied.

Small Contoured Sites

Take a sheet of tracing paper and trace off the individual contours from the ordnance survey map onto a sheet of tracing paper. At two points within the area under consideration two crosses are made as far apart as possible. These are to 'register' the one layer above the other during assembly (see fig. 8). Having decided upon the amount of exaggeration of vertical height to be applied, make a tracing on a piece of cardboard of the lowest contour and mark in the two crosses in the appropriate places. Next, the shape of the contour is cut out with the Stanley knife, and the section of card will then resemble a large piece of jigsaw puzzle. This is glued in its correct place on the baseboard and pins are inserted at the point marked for registering the section. The heads of the pins are cut off leaving the main body of the pins sticking up. The best type of pins are the stainless steel variety sold for dressmaking purposes, not the ordinary office pins as these bend when tapped into a baseboard. Other contours are traced off in sequence and at their point of register a pin hole is made, so that when they are glued into place on top of the lower one, the pieces are threaded over the pins attached to the baseboard so that each contour is in its correct location. When the top layer has been put into place the pins can be pulled out with pliers, or cut off level with the top layer. The assembly should now look like a 'paddy field' with terraces represented by the contours. It can be left like this to give a clean-cut stylised approach to the model, or filled in with plaster of paris, making sure that the cardboard is sprayed with a suitable sealer, otherwise it may swell or distort, after the application of the plaster of paris. The plaster is then sealed after two to three days and painted in the normal way with Cryla colours (see illus. 4).

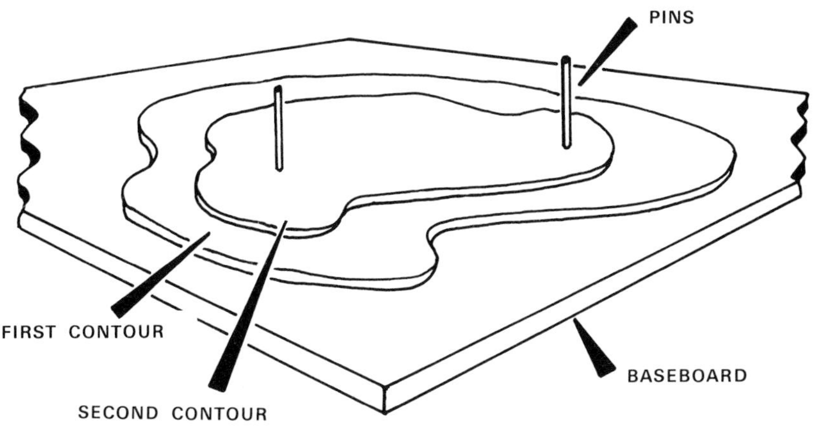

Figure 8

Chapter VI

Constructing houses

When we have a model to construct consisting of a baseboard with buildings, it is often better to leave the baseboard at times in order to construct some of the buildings. By this change the model retains its 'life' as you will not get so tired of an operation which can take sometimes up to two or three days. Houses can be made individually

7. Small detached house, scale 1:100. Trees on adjoining site help set it off to advantage

or, in the case of a repetitive development, a production line technique can be established so that several walls or roof sections can be made together and then stored to await the completion of the other parts.

The majority of models we are dealing with fall into the category of 1 to 100 or 1 to 200 scale, with houses then being 2″ to 3″ square. For this size of house, it is not really necessary to construct them from wood, as cardboard used correctly can be very strong.

Houses made to the scale discussed should not be completely made in the form of 'hollow boxes' for two reasons. It is most important that they do not give an impression of empty shells, and furthermore some internal stressing is necessary to give strength to the construction. One proven method of construction is as follows:

The architect's drawing showing all building elevations is first firmly pinned down to the table or drawing board, and pieces of celluloid or Plexiglas (E) cut to size for each elevation of the building containing windows or glazed doors. The size of celluloid should be so that it is big enough to cover the overall size of *all* windows, etc., but not quite large enough to reach the extremities of the wall sections. The majority of window frames to a new building are either silver or white, so we shall therefore require a drawing pen and a supply of silver paint and photographic white ink. The sections of celluloid should be lightly attached to the plan at the corners with a small piece of Sellotape or adhesive tape, and all window frames are then drawn in with the draughtsman's pen. It is best to draw beyond the actual outside line of the window frames to prevent blobs of ink or paint gathering in the corners and thus destroying realism. All horizontal lines should be drawn first and allowed to thoroughly dry out before attempting to draw the vertical lines. Certain types of transparent material d not take white ink very easily, especially if the tips of the drawing pen are very sharp. If this happens, experiments should be carried out using thinned down poster colours or Cryla colours. Before removing the celluloid from the drawings fix some Sellotape of the correct width to the face of the celluloid to prevent the ink or paint from cracking off as the celluloid is moved. It also gives slightly 'obscure' windows which look more natural than completely clear windows. Removing the celluloid from the drawing, now turn it over and repeat the line of window frames on the back if necessary.

8. Detail of $\frac{1}{8}'' = 1'\ 0''$ model. Old house converted into offices. A case where surrounding property had to be shown in detail

This is not absolutely essential in small scale models, but when windows over 1″ square are being produced, this method gives an impression of individually glazed window frames. The sheets of celluloid are now put aside to await the construction of the walls. At this point a suitable piece of cardboard is selected and by the use of tracing paper or carbon paper the wall size is transferred to the card. All window apertures and door openings should be cut out cleanly with the Stanley knife (Method 1). If the walls are to be painted to represent brick or stone, it is a good idea to give them a first coat of paint around the window and door openings now, as, if this is left until after assembly, a slight slip of the brush can leave paint across the window frames, thus destroying realism (see fig. 9). The pieces of cardboard or polystyrene sheet used for the walls must correspond to the thickness of wall seen in front of the windows or doors, and not to the total scale thickness of the complete wall.

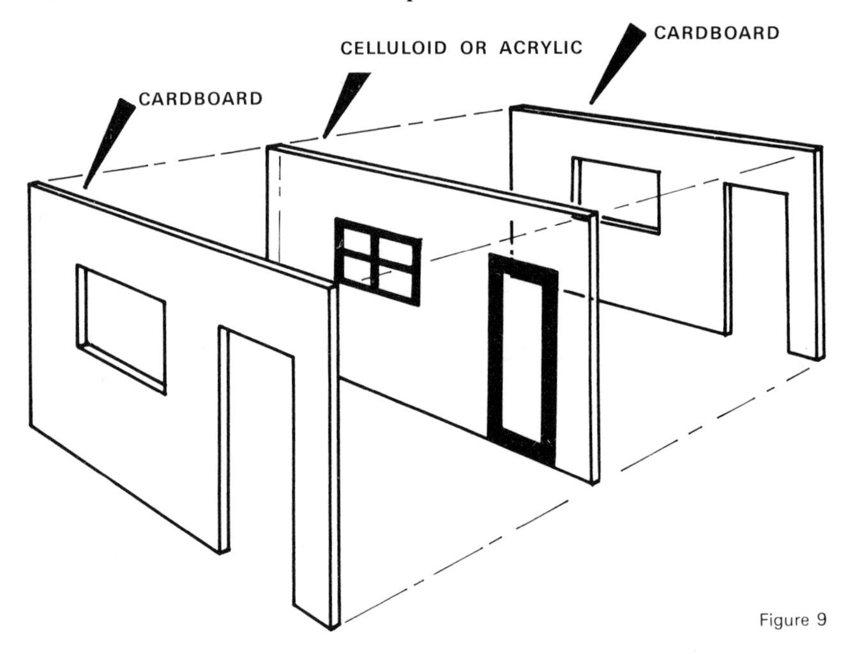

Figure 9

The celluloid sections can now be glued with clear Bostik to the cardboard sections, making sure that no adhesive gets onto the windows (see fig. 10). At this stage the bases of the houses which were temporarily attached to the baseboard can be brought into use, and the one front wall and one end wall can be glued into place.

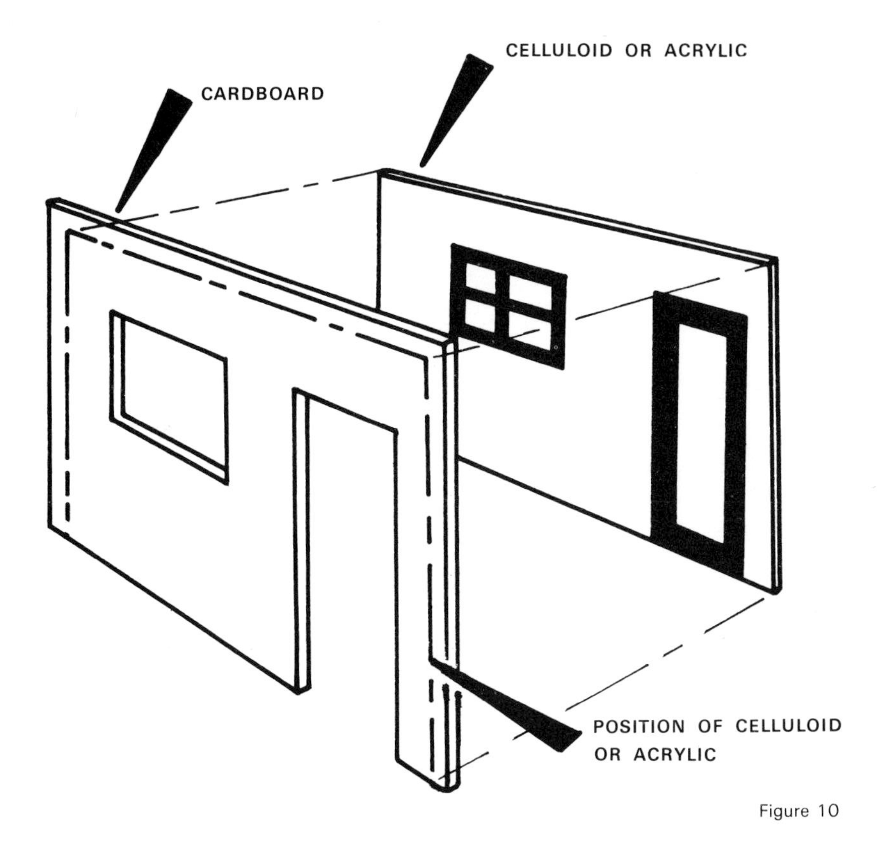

Figure 10

Remember that allowance has been made for the main front wall to overlap the side walls, which will have been cut to the size of the elevation drawing. (If a balsa wood model is being made these difficulties are avoided by 'mitring' the corners of each piece using a scalpel.)

As we don't want a 'hollow' look to the houses on a model, about $\frac{1}{4}''$ or so back from each wall we shall need to fix a section of light grey coloured cardboard behind the window sections. The opportunity can be taken to use these pieces as bracing or strengthening pieces, and after assembly the model will be found to be immensely strong. Continue to assemble the other walls forming the complete house, up to the eaves level. Insert the appropriate masking sections between the walls and then at the centre use a diagonal bracing piece if necessary (see fig. 11).

At this stage the walls have to be painted or covered with brick paper. If the latter, it is a simple matter to trace onto the *back* of the

9. A row of houses can be treated as one unit during construction. Scale $\frac{1}{8}'' = 1'\ 0''$

brick paper the outline of each wall and window opening, then to cut out the sections of paper allowing for an overhang, at each end slightly more than the thickness of the cardboard being used for the model. Use the Stanley knife or scalpel to cleanly cut out the paper sections, and remember to allow sufficient paper at the sides of the window openings to fold over onto the edge of the wall openings after fixing the paper in place. It is not necessary to make an allowance for the bottom of the window openings, as after assembly of the house this will no doubt be covered by a hardwood sill cut from a suitable piece of thin veneer.

If the walls are to be painted then they will need a good coat of Cryla colour mixed to the shade of the particular brick being represented. A general red brick colour can usually be obtained by a mixture of Burnt Umber and Vermillion, but it is wise to experiment on a scrap piece of cardboard before painting the model. After applying the paint, and while it is still wet some indication of brick courses should be made. It is not necessary to faithfully copy every crack and joint in the brickwork, indeed the model would look most unnatural if it were made this way. All that is needed for the brickwork to give a natural appearance is for the tip of the artist's brush to be lightly drawn perfectly horizontally through the paint before it dries. If the model maker's hand is not too steady, a simple tool to help matters is a 3″ cube of wood with a good flat base, with one vertical side covered in sandpaper. The brush is held against this with the thumb and by 'rolling' the brush into position on the block to the desired position, the block can be slid along the working surface

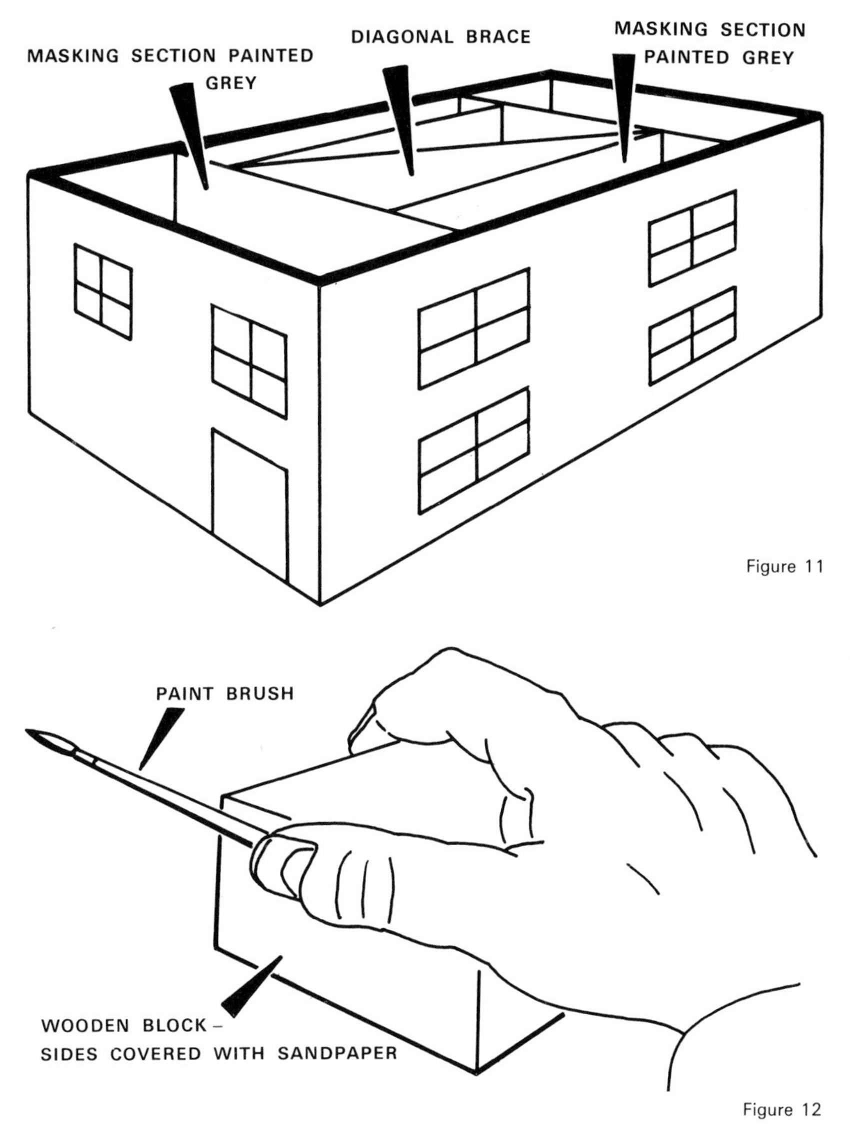

Figure 11

Figure 12

maintaining the brush at the correct, and proper height (see fig. 12). It is essential that the paint used for the main walls is the same shade as the paint which was used for the window openings painted before assembly. If concrete lintels are to be shown on the house these can either be painted on by first masking off the area with Sellotape to give sharp edges, or alternatively pieces of the correct coloured paper can be cut out and stuck on. The window sills can now be cut out and fixed in position and doorsteps can be fashioned from small pieces of balsa wood or stripwood of the correct size.

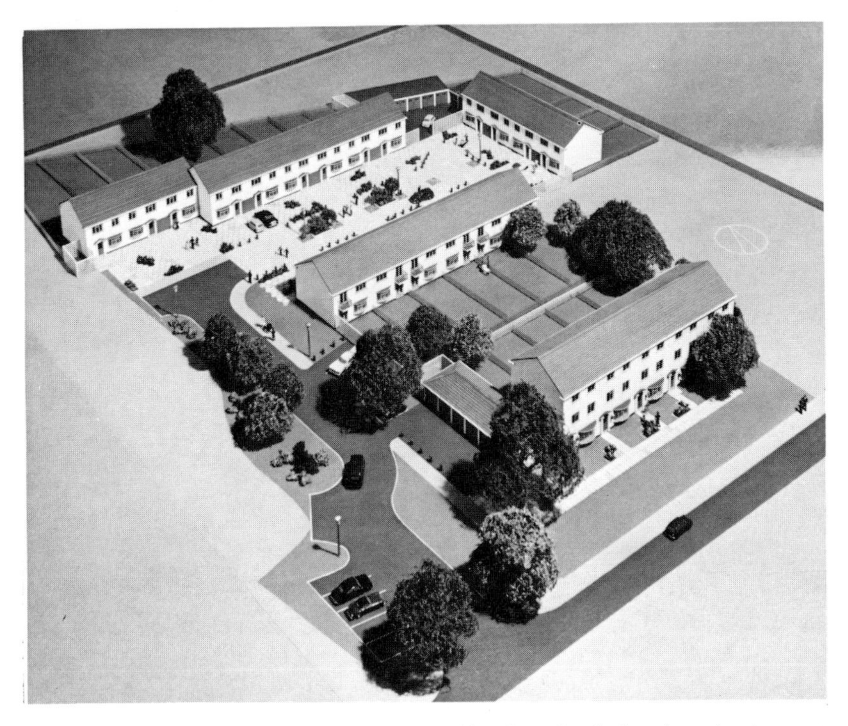

10. Completed housing development model; note particularly grouping of figures

The next stage of construction is to mark out on a piece of cardboard the size of the house base, and then to make a mark surrounding this corresponding to the eaves' overhang, assuming a roof with 'hipped' ends is to be made, or a front and rear only if the house has gable walls extending to the ridge. This piece is cut out and glued into place on the walls and strengthening pieces. Making the roof can be a difficult job unless a drawing is prepared showing a 'projection' of the roof surfaces, as normal front and end elevation drawings do not provide enough reference for a direct measurement to be taken. If this is not possible, the best procedure is to glue into place a section of card representing the correct height of roof and length of ridge taken from the architect's drawing, and then two triangles representing the cross-section of roof (see fig. 13). A piece of card, cut to the length of the roof at the eaves, is then placed against the ridge: make two marks where the ends of the ridge touch the card. When these points are joined up to the extremities of the card the correct shape of the roof is apparent. This operation is repeated on the other side of the roof and both sections are glued into place. It is then a very simple matter to take direct measurements for the roof ends, cut them out and fix them into position. The construction of the roof is finished off by cutting thin strips of balsa wood to length and fixing them into place at the junction of the roof sections with the eaves to represent gutters. The roof is next painted using the guide block for the paint brush as for the painting of the walls and finally ridge tiles are added by taking a strip of paper and curving it along the length to cover up the junction of the cardboard sections (see fig. 14).

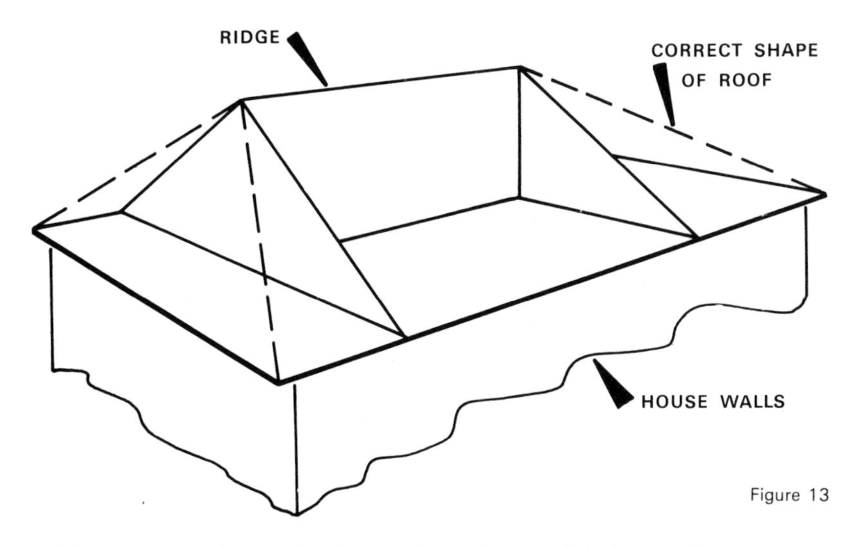

Figure 13

The construction of chimneys is quite straightforward. These are made from cardboard or polystyrene sheet, making sure that the 'V' slot in the base corresponds *exactly* to the profile of the roof. A cardboard capping is made and sections of the correct size dowel rod are cut and inserted to represent chimneys (fig. 15). A final touch is the use of cooking foil or silver paper to represent 'lead flashing' and if

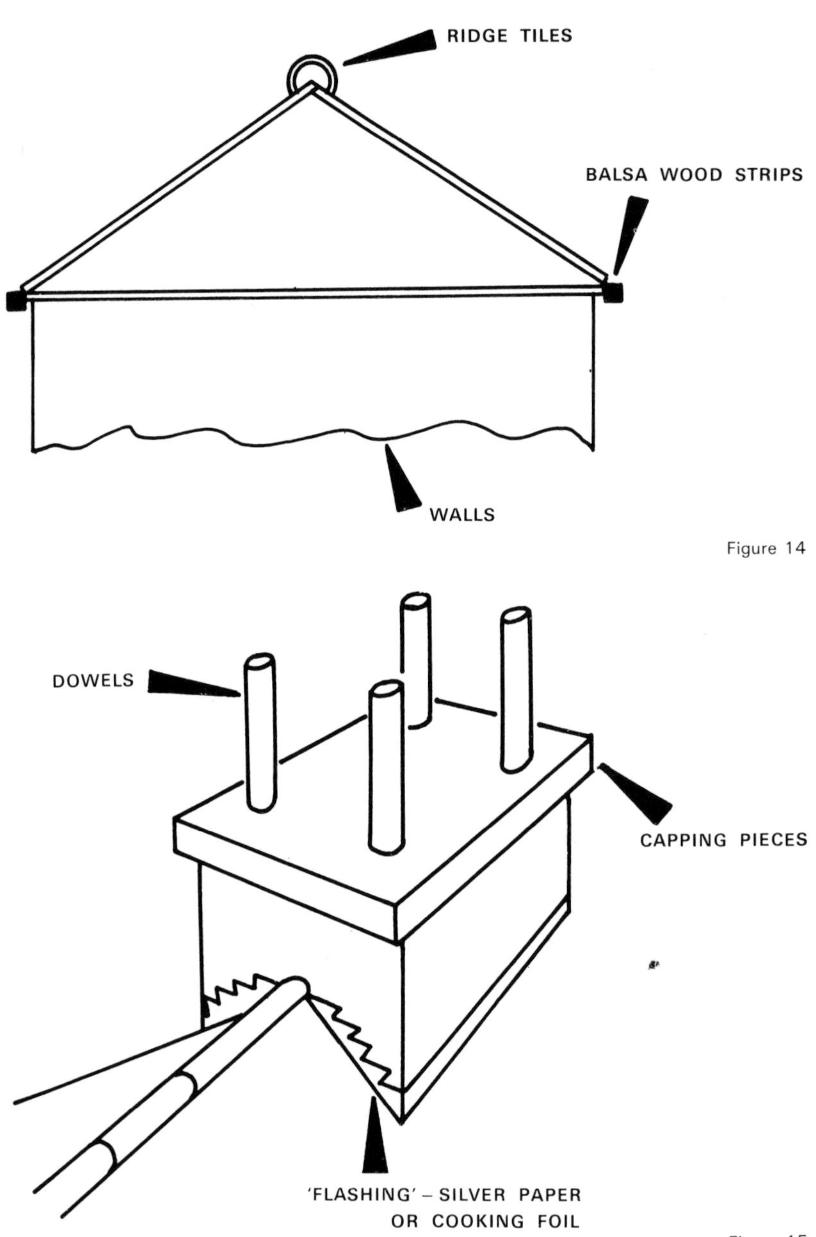

Figure 14

Figure 15

serrations are cut into this, they must be spaced correctly to correspond to the brick courses to scale, otherwise realism is lost.

If the house being constructed has gable ends to the walls, then it will become necessary to construct 'bargeboards' to finish off the ends of the roof. These are made by placing the assembled house complete with roof on a piece of card, and then marking from this the correct angle of roof. The bargeboard is drawn to the correct scale width inside this inverted 'V' and the gutter ends to the correct shapes are marked out. After cutting out with the Stanley knife the cards ends are glued into position. Rainwater downpipes can be made either from stiff florists' wire though this bends rather easily, or from the wire rods sold for electric welding processes by an engineering materials supplier. This is sold in cut lengths, is very stiff and is available in two or three different thicknesses; short pieces can also be hammered into the baseboard to form posts or poles.

Chapter VII

Garages and workshops

A garage model usually consists of workshop, sales room, toilets, petrol pump islands, their canopy, and landscaping. The construction of the actual workshop is generally of a clear span building with walls of a suitable brick, or asbestos sheeting, with doors (big enough to take vehicles), of the roller-shutter, collapsing or 'up-and-over' type.

11. Petrol-filling station model during construction. Canopy removed

When making a scale model of such a building it is simpler to follow the system laid down by the specialist building suppliers, namely to cut out a series of frames from card or plywood, erect these on the base, suitably spaced, and then construct roof sheets to cover them. The walls and windows are made in a similar manner to houses, and fitted into place between the building frames, leaving correctly placed door openings (see fig. 16). These of course can be in the ends or sides of the building, depending on the planned layout.

If the vehicle entrance doors are to give the impression of aluminium they can be made of cardboard covered in cooking foil, suitably scored with a knife to represent corrugations or panels. When the doors are of the 'folding-sliding' or 'concertina' type, before gluing the aluminium foil to the cardboard, the cardboard should be scored vertically on alternate sides and bent slightly at the score marks to give the impression of a folding door. A development of this idea is to actually fold the door for approximately half its width so that when assembled on the model it will give a certain amount of visibility into the workshop. If a small model vehicle of the correct scale is shown entering or leaving via this door, then it will serve to indicate the movement of traffic intended by the designer of the site. Roller-shutter doors are made by a similar method, but in this case the scoring or marking is carried out on the face of the cooking foil to represent slats, and the door, if shown partly open, must be in a raised position for the full width of the opening.

Any roof ventilators on the model can be carved from balsa wood, or fabricated from thin cardboard and glued into place; it must be remembered however, that if they are open type cowls they should be painted matt black on the inside before attaching.

If name boards appear on the building it is very difficult to give a realistic appearance if they are hand painted. There are several types of transfer letters on the market under various trade names which can be obtained in black, white, red, blue, or yellow, in a variety of type faces, but after fixing to the cardboard they should be given two or three coats of the correct fixative.

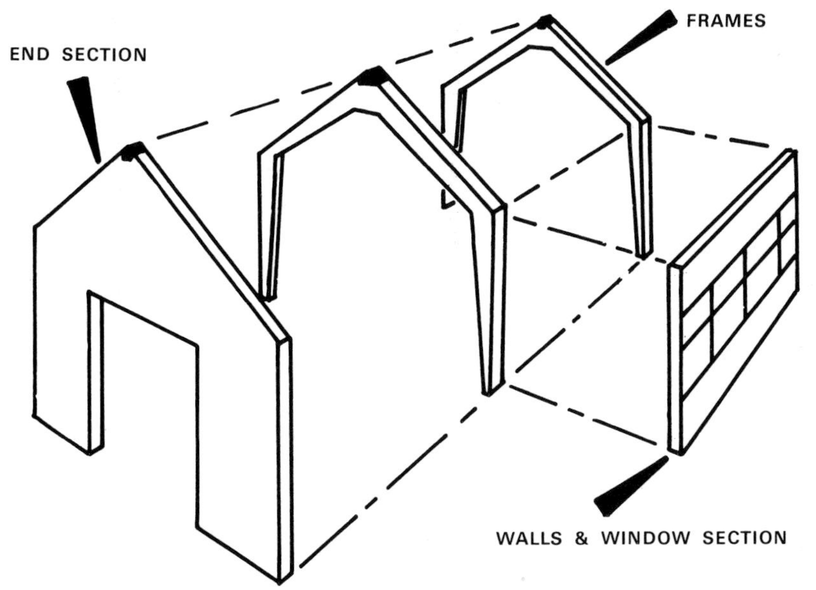

Figure 16

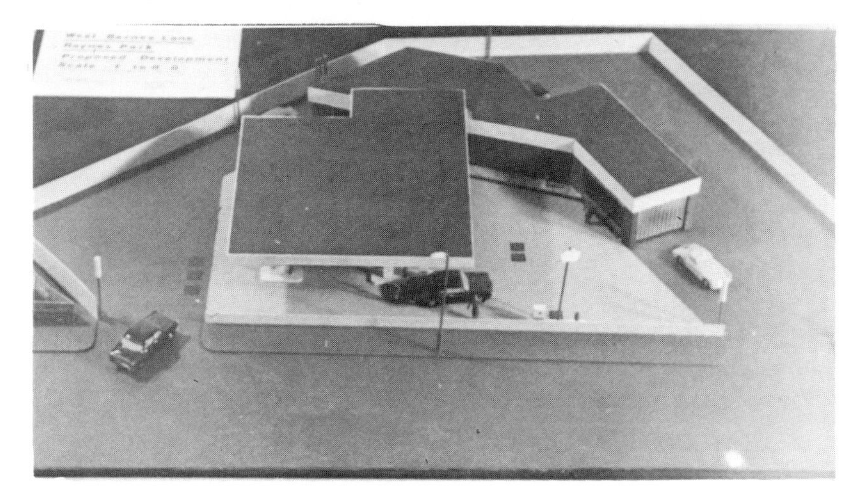

12. Standard size canopy and building on an irregularly shaped site. Scale $\frac{1}{8}'' = 1'\ 0''$

The construction of the sales room and toilets should generally follow the procedure laid down for house construction, except that as larger glazed areas are involved with showroom windows, internal stiffening sections are not always possible except in the toilets. More of the interior is also visible, so coloured paper should be used to cover the walls where a decorated finish is desired, and also on the floor, suitably marked out in squares to represent tiles. It is also necessary to indicate counters or shelving by strips of card in order to avoid a blank empty look to the building. Usually the roof of these buildings is flat and is covered in black roofing felt with a black waterproofing process and chippings. A good representation of this finish can be obtained by the use of a suitable grade of black emery-paper known as 'wet or dry'. This is available in sheets from most hardware stores and is sold for the purpose of rubbing down paintwork on motor car panels during the re-finishing process. Several grades are obtainable, ranging from very coarse to very smooth. Medium grade is the best for the purpose mentioned, but a small stock of a fairly coarse grade should also be obtained as it has many uses and can even be painted to give a 'pebble-dash' or roughcast surface to buildings. Most garage sales rooms and kiosks also have white wooden fascia boards extending the width of the building and continuing along the sides. These can be cut from white polystyrene sheet to the full width, scored with the Stanley knife to the correct width of planking. The score marks are then filled with diluted black ink and the surplus ink is wiped off. This process creates a very realistic effect of painted planking, and can also be used to represent close boarded timber cladding on the face of buildings.

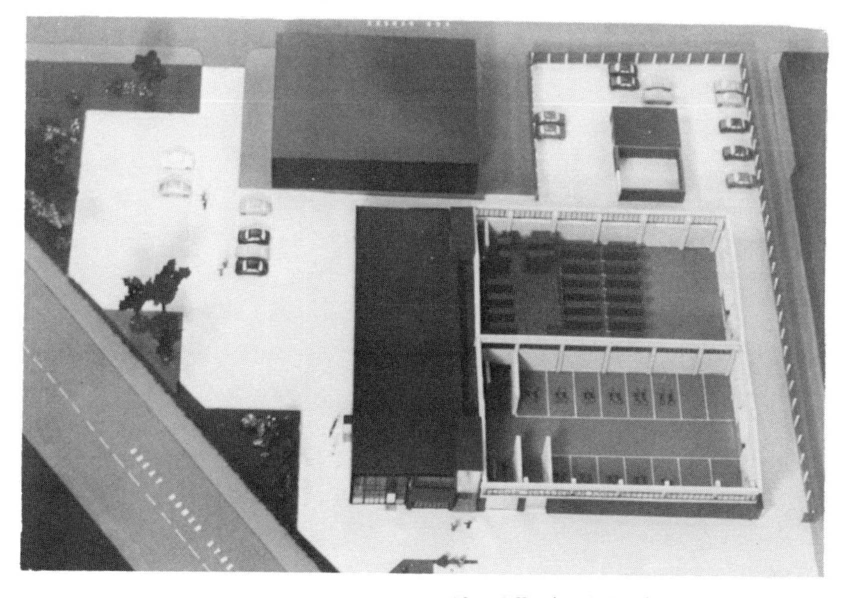

13. Office/workshop/warehouse model. Scale 1:150. Roof section removable to reveal internal layout. *John Wallwork Ltd., Manchester*

The canopy extending over the petrol pumps is usually flat, supported on four- or six-column supports. In model form this is the weakest part of the structure and is therefore much more liable to damage in use or transit. The upright supports should be made from lengths of welding rod hammered into the baseboard in a perfectly upright position, then painted before the canopy top is placed into position. The top is best made from hardboard, cut to shape with a fine-toothed saw to prevent ragged edges, it is faced below with white polystyrene sheet or thin cardboard. The position of the supporting columns should be marked through with a scriber point, so that they line up with the supporting columns on the baseboard. The top of the canopy is covered with a suitable grade of 'wet and dry' emery-paper, and to complete the construction the canopy is edged with a narrow strip of white polystyrene sheet to represent the white painted edging.

Any petrol company name can be added to the edging before fixing into place. The canopy is attached to the supporting columns by tapping it into place on the wire supports which have previously been filed to a blunt point for this purpose. A strip of card marked off at the correct scale height of the canopy is used to ensure that the canopy is correctly positioned (see fig. 17). Obviously, before the canopy is placed in position all work should be completed below it, such as the fixing of petrol pumps, cars, figures, etc., and the painting of the concreted area around the pump islands.

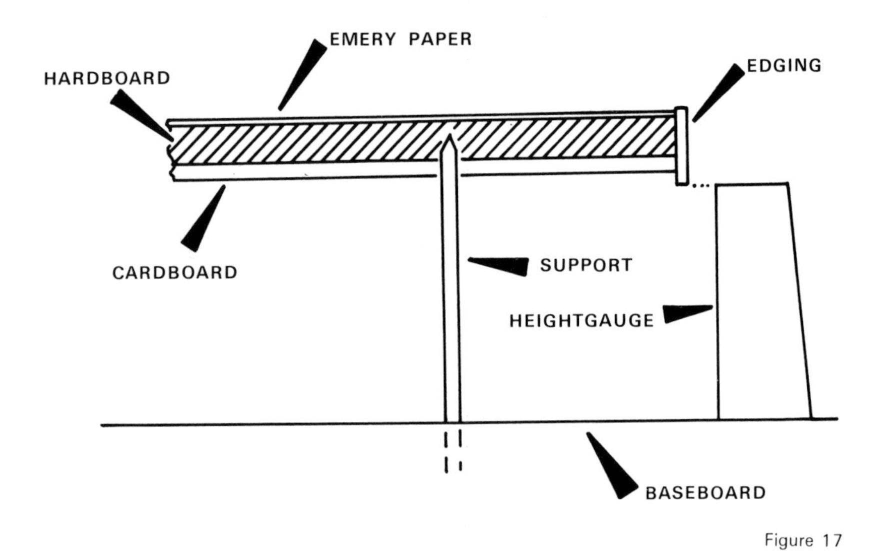

Figure 17

Welding wire can also be used to represent the 'breather' pipes to the underground petrol storage tanks, but if possible use the spokes of an old bicycle wheel. They have the advantage of being turned over at the hub end, and when painted give a very good impression of weatherproof cowls; it is also a simple matter to hammer them into place as they are not liable to bend. A guide hole should first be drilled into the baseboard to locate them before they are placed in position, and a dab of clear Bostik put on the bottom before tapping into place.

A model garage can have the whole effect ruined if the petrol pumps are not carefully finished off. The modern type of petrol pump is lower and wider than the old type, so needs to be made with great accuracy. For the smaller scale of 1 to 200 or 1″ = 16′ 0″ it is only necessary to carve the petrol pump out of a solid piece of wood, or fabricate it from four pieces of white polystyrene or cardboard (see fig. 18). The various positions where the gallonage and price appear on the dial, and the petrol company insignia on the base together with any other details are marked on with a fine mapping pen and ink. For the larger scale of 1 to 100 or 1″ = 8′ 0″ the unit is still built up from sections, but the head of the petrol pump is surrounded by white card (visiting cards or postcards are the correct thickness), and after marking the face of the dial, it can be covered in thin clear celluloid or even Sellotape to give the appearance of a glazed front.

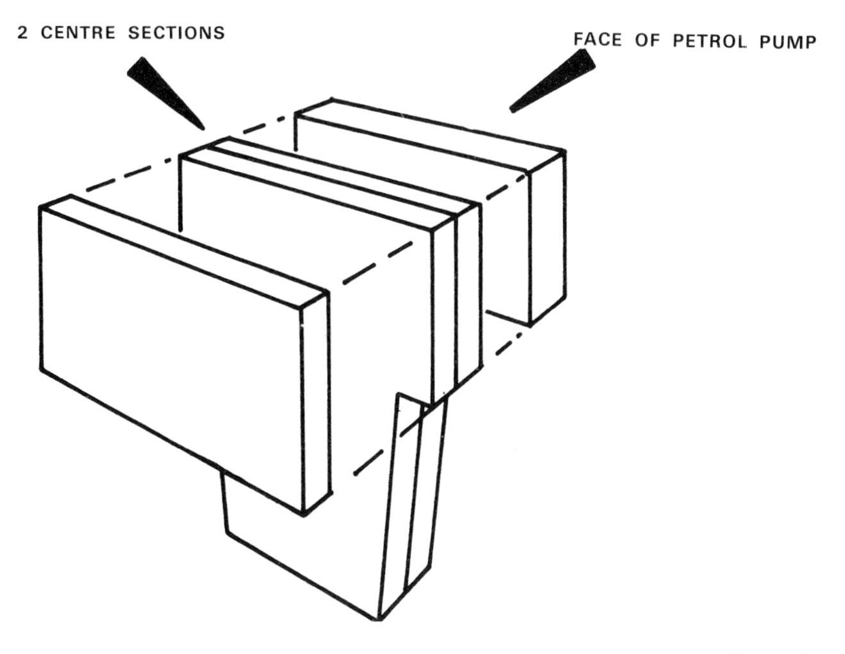

Figure 18

The garage layout is completed by erecting boundary fences and walls. If 'ranch-style' fencing is used as per current practice, these should be made from white polystyrene sheet with black lines drawn on to indicate the gaps between the boards, with small sections of white painted balsa wood glued on to simulate posts. Most modern garages also have 'Stick' lights around the boundaries consisting of tube lighting in a casing attached to a pole. These are quite easy to make, ball-point re-fills yield a good supply of small-bore plastic tubing which is cut to length then glued on to a length of welding rod hammered into the baseboard. Using a revolving-head leather punch a small circle of card is produced and glued to the top as a capping piece, then the whole unit is painted white. The welding rod is hammered into the base *before* fixing the plastic tubing into place, otherwise the light may get damaged (see fig. 19).

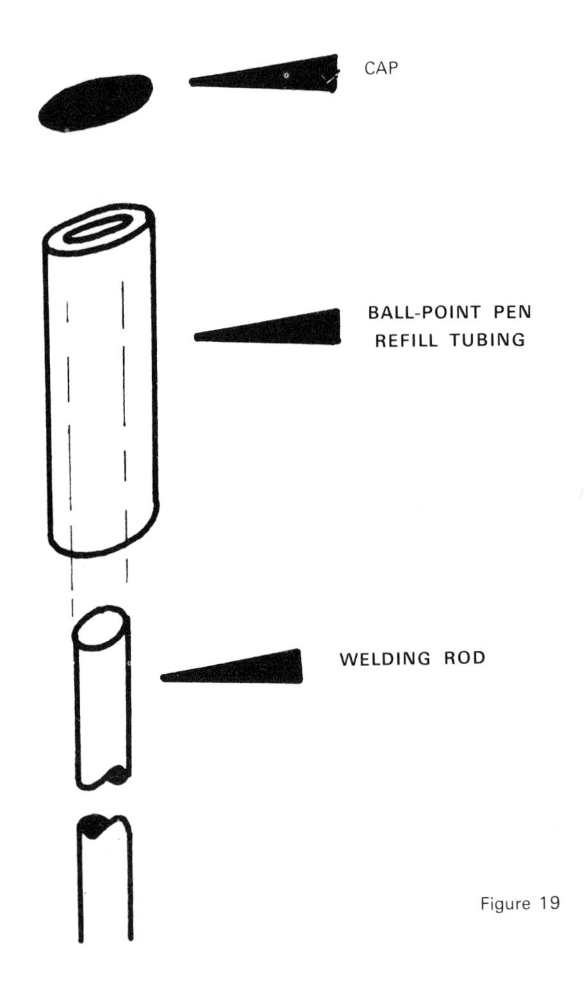

Figure 19

Chapter VIII

Multi-storey buildings; shops and shopping precincts

Multi-storey buildings

Once a model gets to be higher than 2 or 3 inches the danger of damage in handling increases considerably, so tall buildings need a stronger form of construction, although from the exterior appearance this is not always apparent. Give strength to these structures by constructing them around a block of wood securely glued to a baseboard; screws can be inserted from below for added strength (see fig. 20).

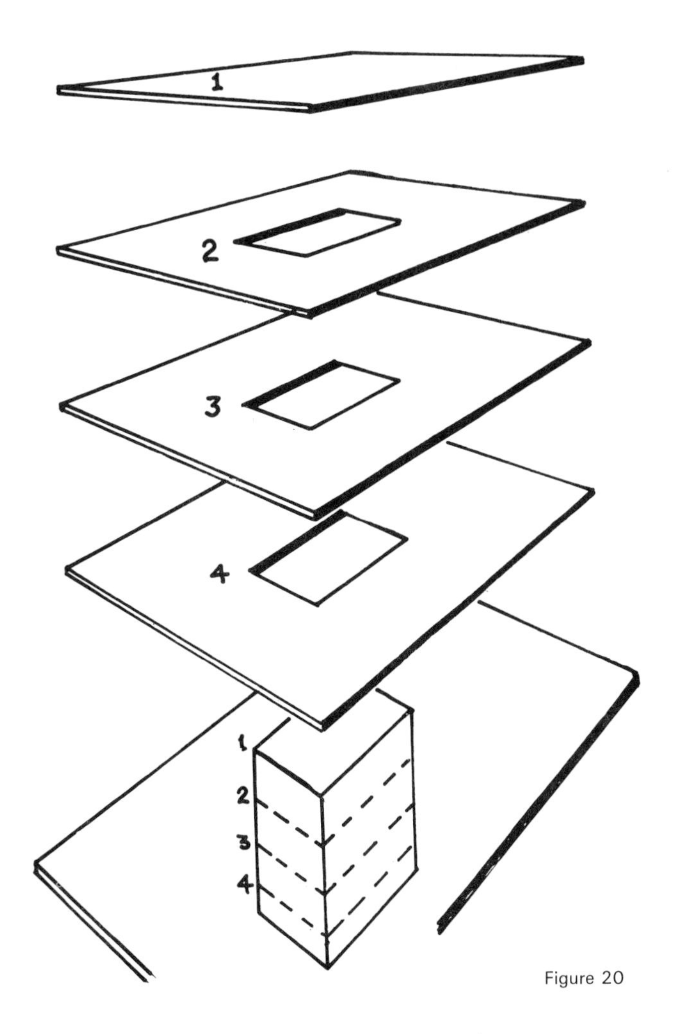

Figure 20

14. Multi-storey office block constructed
on a solid core around a central courtyard

The method of construction for an office block or block of flats can proceed in the manner described for houses regarding the general procedure of marking out windows, etc. Each floor of the building must however, have a square hole cut into it corresponding to the size of the wooden strengthening block, and during assembly of the various walls the intermediate floors are glued into position. The wooden block should be painted grey before the assembled building is lowered into position over the block, and this does away with any necessity for intermediate strengthening pieces unless the multi-storey building is of such an area that by looking through the windows it is possible to see beyond the block of wood.

Sometimes several blocks of wood are needed where lift shafts or staircases would appear in the actual building. It then becomes necessary to insert strengthening pieces between the various floors to act as baffles (see fig. 20). The length of the wooden block should be of such a dimension that when the building is lowered over it, the top of the block reaches the underside of the flat roof. If a pitched roof is part of the building, then the top of the block should be shaped to give a good fit to the underside of the roof.

15. Shopping centre model with 'Tower Restaurant'. The tower must be rigidly fixed into baseboard

When working to a scale of 1 to 100 or greater then it is possible to assemble the building floor by floor with the strengthening sections arranged in the correct position of the dividing walls on the individual floors. Where a lift shaft or section of air-conditioning trunking runs through all the floors, then this will be constructed in short sections with the ends painted matt black or shaded to represent a cross-section taken through each piece. The floors are then not glued to each other but are placed one above the other using the wooden blocks as 'locating pieces' so that anyone interested in the interior of the building can see how the individual floors are laid out. In an office block for instance, each floor can have the divisions to the offices arranged in a different sequence on each floor so that a client can select the arrangement he requires to suit his particular set of circumstances.

Every multi-storey building having a flat roof must be finished off by paying particular attention to the flat roof itself. 'Wet-or-dry' emery-paper is used to give the characteristic effect to the cardboard used to construct the roof, and it is most important that any structure on the roof such as winding-gear for lifts, water tanks, etc., should be placed in their correct relative position. If the roof is made to lift off then locating blocks must be fixed to the corners to slide inside the corners of the top floor to maintain the roof in its correct position.

If the building being constructed is a block of flats, with each floor identical, then it is not necessary to make the floors so that they lift off. Making a complete wall based on a single sheet of celluloid or perspex is obviously easier than a lot of separate sections, instead of this it is suggested that a larger scale model is constructed quite separately of an actual floor. An ideal scale is 1 to 50 or $\frac{1}{4}'' = 1'\ 0''$ as at this enlarged scale it is possible to show a great deal of detail without handling too many tiny pieces of wood, wire, or cardboard. To start with, the $\frac{1}{4}''$ scale plan is drawn on the prepared base, and a special note is made of where bathrooms and kitchens appear, as the floor tiles must be the first part to be tackled. Assuming that the model being constructed is for a multi-storey block of flats, each floor having two single-bedroomed flats, and two two-bedroomed flats. Each flat will have a kitchen, dining room, and bathroom and entrance hall in addition to bedroom or bedrooms. When the main entrance lobby common to all flats is included this will give a total of 23 'compartments' on a baseboard roughly 24″ square so it will be appreciated that 1 to 50 or $\frac{1}{4}'' = 1'\ 0''$ is about the smallest scale that can comfortably be used for this type of model.

It will usually be found in practice that all kitchens and bathrooms are grouped together to simplify the design of the building, so this total area is noted on the marked out baseboard. Next having selected the colour for the floor tiles, say light green and white mottled, light green and white paint are squeezed out onto the pallet. The light green

16. Individual floors lift off to facilitate interior planning. Scale 1:100

paint is then applied to the floor area using 'dabbing' movements rather than stroking the paint brush along. This is immediately followed up by 'dabbing' white paint onto the green, the result being a very pleasing mottled green and white finish. When dry, the painted area is ruled off into perfect squares to the scale size of the tiles, using a very hard pencil such as a grade 6H. The appearance now is of a tiled, mottled floor.

The next operation is to cut out each wall section, starting with the extra thick cavity walls dividing off individual flats. These walls are built up from three layers of card or white polystyrene sheet with the inner layers of card or white polystyrene sheet with the inner sheet stopping short of the top by about $\frac{1}{4}$″. When viewed from above then the appearance is obtained of a cavity wall. The individual partition walls are cut out to the drawing making sure that all doorways are to the same standard size. The pieces cut out of the doorways are put aside for future use as doors. Where a wall butts up to another wall, the position should be marked using a set-square, so that assembly will be simplified. Remember always to work from the inside towards the outside, with the outside walls being the last items to be fitted, otherwise difficulty will be experienced fitting the various pieces. Assemble each flat in turn before gluing it down to the baseboard, and as a detail add skirting boards and architraves around doorways cut out from visiting cards. All partition walls are now glued into place (see fig. 21). It will probably be noticed that the floor tiles extend some of the way into the other rooms, this doesn't matter as the floors are to be 'carpeted' and will cover up an over-run!

The carpets are very simple to make. Get a supply of white 'flock' paper and cut to the exact size of the individual rooms. Paint it with diluted Cryla colour and glue into place. Generally, flock paper should be used for carpets and curtains as fabrics look wrong, particularly for curtains where folding occurs because the folds are never 'to scale'. An exception is where patterned carpets are called for: it will be found that some neckties are thin enough to be used as carpets, but care must be taken to cut the material cleanly, and a small all-over pattern must be selected so that it is to scale!

The sections of cardboard cut out from the walls or partitions are now brought into use as doors. If hardwood veneered doors are required, then real or 'full-size' veneers cannot be used, as their grain is not to scale. Instead, use should be made of catalogues or leaflets obtainable from timber merchants, there are several issued showing printed fascimiles of wood grains, these are quite close enough to be used to this scale. The doors are glued into place in the half-opened

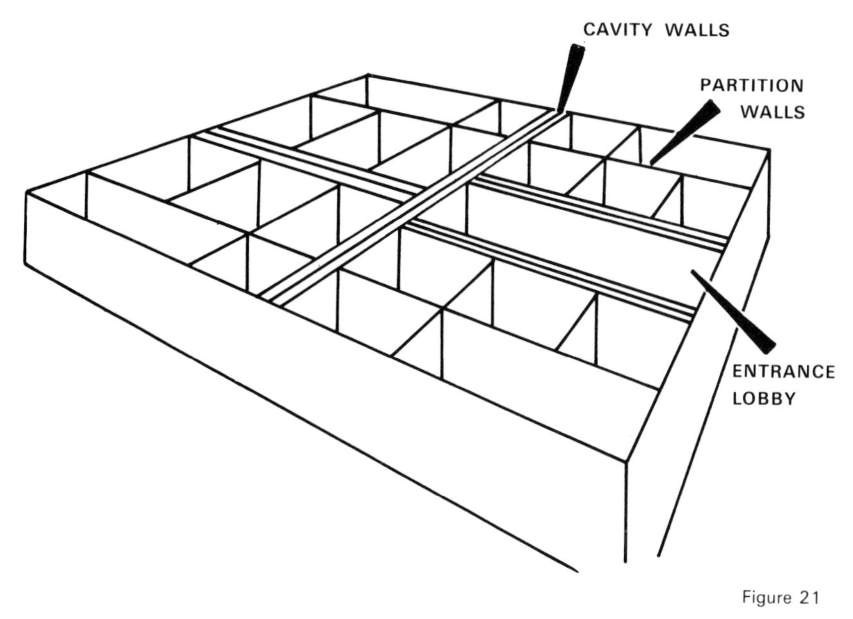

Figure 21

position, this serves to illustrate the opening of the door, and also helps to stiffen the partitions; the edges of the cardboard must be painted brown to match the veneers before gluing into place.

The fittings for bathroom and kitchen are all obtainable from a model-makers' supply company (see p. 85) and are not worth the time and trouble spent trying to make them individually. The working surfaces and cupboards can be constructed from card and printed veneers, similar to the doors and fixed into place. Internal shelves in the cupboards can be made from thin cardboard and the sliding doors are then glued in the half-open position. If a hot-water cylinder is to be shown in the airing cupboard, then this is very easily constructed from a suitable piece of dowel rod. The model gets to be too 'fussy' if an attempt is made to show every pipe leading out of the airing cupboard, an *indication* of what it actually is, is all that is required.

The last operation is to erect the outside walls and balconies, etc. To give some protection to the model, the baseboard should be big enough to leave 1″–2″ around the outside walls when complete. This surround together with the edge moulding itself should be given two coats of matt black paint, thus showing that the floor area in question is not on the ground. Of course, if the $\frac{1}{4}''$ scale model of the typical floor area of the block of flats is the *ground* floor and entrance hall, then the idea of the matt black will not apply. Instead, an indication of landscaping should be included.

Shops and shopping precincts

A model of a shopping precinct is often required to give planning officers a good idea of how a shop front or standardised shop design will look when built adjacent to other buildings of an older design. Many nation-wide multiple stores have a standardised design which does not always fit into its surroundings, and in addition to these there are individual shops which have very unconventional ideas of what the appearance of their premises should look like. Producing a model of the shopping development, and adding details of the individual shops as they are sold or leased, serves to give an excellent impression to potential tenants of how their premises will look in relation to their neighbours.

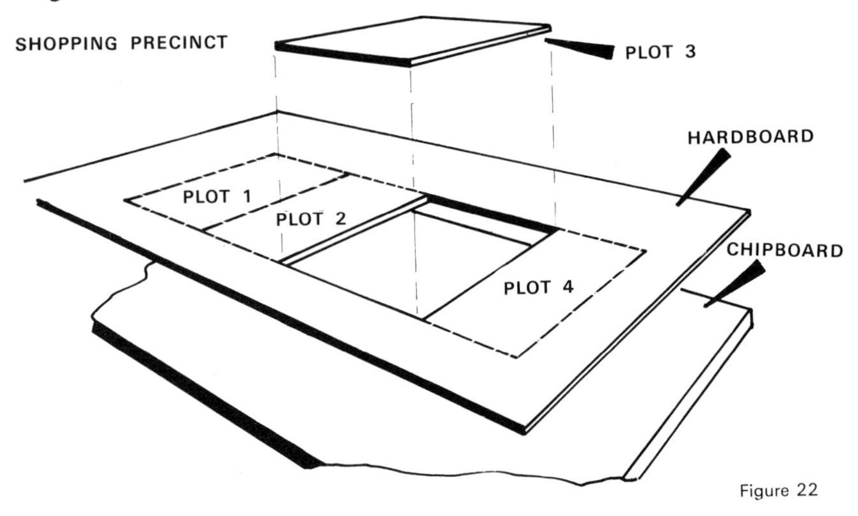

Figure 22

The baseboard is prepared by obtaining a section of $\frac{1}{2}''$ chipboard to the size required, and a piece of $\frac{1}{8}''$ hardboard to the same size. The hardboard will form the bases of the individual shops, so it is given two coats of hardboard primer or emulsion paint, and the plan of the area is reproduced on it, with either tracing paper or carbon paper. The shops are given numbers, either true numbers corresponding to the site numbers allocated by the developer, or failing this, a sequence of numbers or letters is used by the model maker, these being marked on the reference plan. The next operation is to drill a very fine pin-hole in the corner of one shop plot, thread the blade of a fretsaw through it and cut out the individual shop bases (see fig. 22).

If the shopping precinct is on different levels, these will have to be modelled using different sheets of hardboard, depending on the amount of change in ground level occurring on the site. The hardboard surrounding the shop bases can then be glued to the actual chipboard base, leaving holes where the shops will eventually be built. The advantage of this system is that the shops can all be constructed as open-fronted 'shells' and details added as the various units are leased out or sold.

The baseboard is now marked out and painted to show paved areas, trees, flower beds, seats, figures, etc., and in fact at this early stage in the model all landscaping can be completed. The shops are now constructed in 'shell' form, that means with the dividing walls only, but if there are flats above the shops or store rooms these can be constructed on the same principle as straightforward house construction (see fig. 23). The outside of the walls dividing the shops from each other should be painted matt black as these will eventually abutt to form a continuous line of shops.

It might be decided at this stage of the proceedings that lighting will be installed in the model. If this is the case then batteries will have to be stored in the roof space, or the flats above the shops. The question

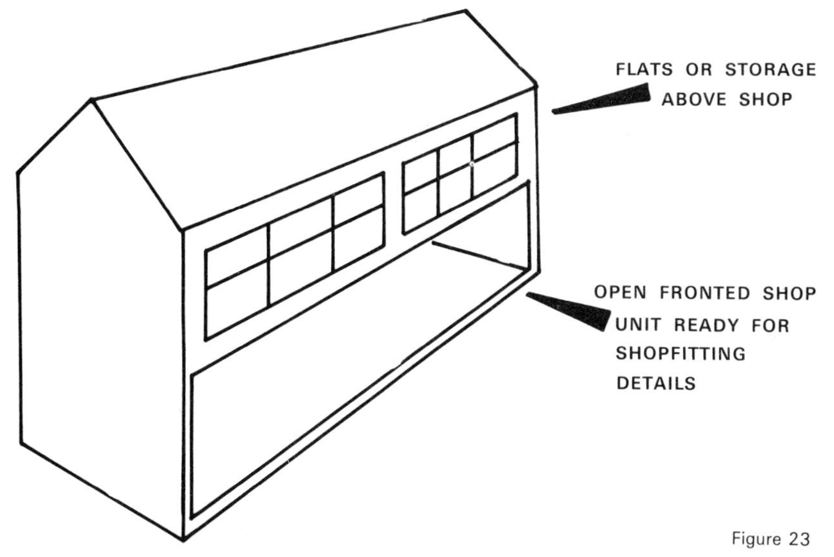

Figure 23

of lighting is fully dealt with on pp. 96/100, sufficient to state now that provision must be made for the roof or rear wall to be capable of removal for access to the batteries.

As shopfitting details are received, so the individual shop fronts can be constructed. Extensive use can be made here of coloured perspex or coloured plastic sheeting obtained from old toys or discarded kitchen utensils! It is also a very good opportunity to use glossy card obtained from brochures and catalogues from exhibitions or large department stores where these items are more readily available. Any lettering or names fixed to the fascia board of the shop should be constructed from transfer lettering as the lettering must be very precise, and hand-written fascia boards are not generally acceptable. Very often a shop front has to be made using a distinctive trade mark or easily recognisable emblem of the particular firm (see p. 102). The company's letter heading or literature will usually produce one suitable for the purpose; it should be cut out very carefully and a small section of Plexiglas or celluloid attached to the front of it.

It will be necessary to use a thicker grade of Plexiglas for shop windows (with a thin grade stresses may occur where it is attached due to temperature changes and these can cause it to buckle or bulge in the middle). Great care must also be taken when drawing the edges of the window frames; it is sometimes better to cut out very thin strips of card of a suitable colour, and glue them into place. Again, due to the relatively large area of window, the interior of the shop should be constructed in sufficient detail to indicate counters, display cases, window display, staging, etc. The floors and walls can be covered with suitable coloured paper or painted in the correct colours. Doors should be fixed in the half-open position to give some circulation of air to the interior of the shop, to prevent distortion or condensation as the materials dry out.

Several small figures should be obtained from the specialist suppliers and fixed in position to give life to the model (Appendix C). They should not be scattered around singly, but fixed in groups. If there is a focal point such as an ornamental fountain or flower bed in the shopping precinct then the figures could be shown congregating in this locality. In addition to giving a more natural look to the model, the grouping of figures also simplifies the question of removing the various shop sections for inspection or construction purposes.

Modern shopping precincts are usually built on the same principle, often with a covered verandah or covered pavement linking up all the shops with a covered cross-over section so that shoppers can cross from one bank of shops to the other without getting wet if it is raining (see page 57). When a model of this sort of development is being made, the common covered way should be made in one section and attached to the main baseboard, and *not* made in individual pieces for each shop. The advantage to this method of construction is that extra stability is given to the completed model and also that the various shops do not have a protruding section attached to them when they are removed from the baseboard. In addition to these advantages, when all the shops are completed and finally assembled on the baseboard, the joints between them are not noticed, whereas a series of joints appearing on the covered walk-way would give a very untidy appearance to the completed model.

17. One floor of a block of flats. All rooms are identifiable. Scale $\frac{1}{4}''$ = 1′ 10″

Chapter IX

Old and historic buildings

Time does not stand still, and new buildings have to be designed and built in areas where probably for hundreds of years no changes have taken place. An architect designs a building to satisfy his clients' requirements as to usage, but at the same time it must be designed and built using modern materials that yet fit in with the surroundings. These may consist of old buildings that have matured and mellowed with age, and the only way a proposed new building can be shown as part of a locality is for the old buildings surrounding it to be faithfully reproduced in model form.

Much more time spent on the site must be allowed for obtaining reference for the old building model, as in very few cases are drawings available. Obviously it is not possible to accurately measure every building or wall, but what is called for is an eye for proportion. Measurements can usually be taken along a curb or boundary wall or building, and measurements taken vertically can reach to the top of a doorway or window. From these accurate dimensions it is a simple matter of calculating the height of a building from an assessment made of the number of times the known dimension divides into the height being calculated. A check for accuracy should be made frequently during the sketching stage so that correct proportions are maintained. It must be remembered that the spaces between buildings are just as important as the buildings themselves. At least one diagonal should be included in the sketch elevation as it serves to show if it runs through the corner of a window for instance on the ground floor, and then perhaps continues through the centre of an upper floor. This method can also be very useful in working out the height of trees or poles near the buildings being modelled, as a 'sight' line taken through a building will meet a tree or pole at a point which can easily be calculated (see fig. 24).

It helps to take photographs of old buildings from all possible angles, including some colour slides for reference to the actual shades of brickwork, and roof tiles on the buildings. If colour slides are taken from far enough away to prevent distortion in the camera lens, they can be projected onto a sheet of squared paper or graph paper and the outline of the most important features traced off onto the paper so that the judging of window sizes or other proportions is dispensed with. Fairly accurate front and side elevation drawings can easily be produced by this means, as most slide projectors can be accurately focused to produce a clear picture on a sheet of paper 20″–24″ wide.

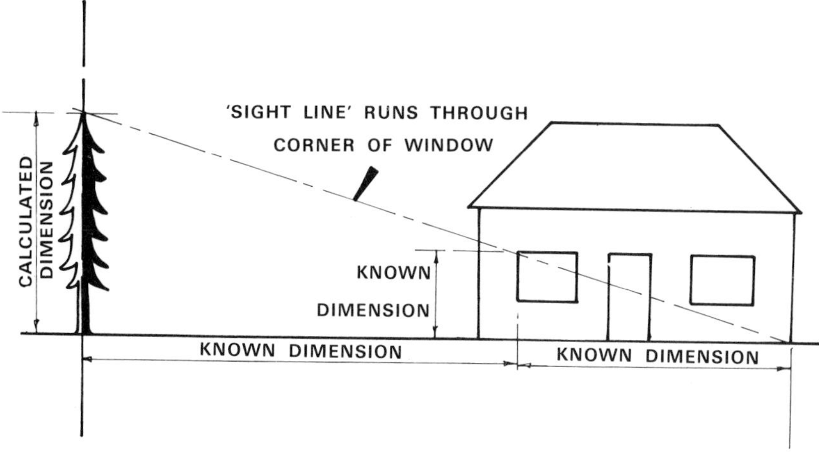

Figure 24

As previously stated, old buildings have walls which are usually anything but flat and consistent in thickness. This must be kept in mind when making them in model form, as any old building made with sharp edges and clean-cut features tends to look too much like a stage-setting, and destroys the whole basis of the idea that they are to emphasise the way a new development fits in with an old neighbourhood.

Probably the best scale to work in is $\frac{1}{8}'' = 1'\ 0''$ or 1 to 100 as model railway brick papers, etc., can be used as a basis for the wall coverings. The method of constructing the buildings generally follows the method for making new houses; but after a close study of the photographs or actual buildings a decision must be made where corners are worn away, or roof lines sag or are distorted with age. These points can be pared away very carefully with a Stanley knife, taking care that the walls are not cut through completely to weaken the structure of the model. If the depth of the 'worn corner' is greater than the thickness of card originally selected for the walls then sheets of soft cardboard or balsa wood must be built up on the inside of the corners and any other places before starting to cut away. Waterproof glue is next used in a dilute form, all wall surfaces are carefully painted over with this, and thin tissue paper is placed on and 'patted' into place. More coats of waterproof glue and tissue are applied over the tissue paper until the walls have taken on the desired irregular appearance. Emphasis is placed on the use of waterproof glue so that when it is dry and 'cured' in place with the tissue paper it will not be subsequently affected by the paste which will be used for the application of the brick paper.

The next operation requires great care and should not be tackled if the model maker is feeling tired or hurried. This is the use of brick paper to give the finish to the outside of the walls. A sheet of brick patterned paper, slightly larger than the area to be covered, is chosen and the borders are cut off. It is now wet thoroughly and then put aside for five minutes or so for the surplus water to drain away. The paper *and* the surface of the wall to be covered next receive an application of paste, and the brick paper is placed in position. The object of wetting the paper before pasting is so that it can be stretched over the uneven surface of the walls, and if brick courses on the actual building have run 'out of true', this can be reproduced in the model by carefully pulling the brick paper into position. It cannot be over emphasised that this wet paper must be handled very carefully to avoid tearing or splitting. An examination of the building or photographs will usually show staining or discolouration of the brickwork under overflow pipes or broken rain gutters, etc. The area immediately below window sills or other projections is also a different shade to the rest of the brickwork. Cryla paints or watercolours mixed very thinly can be used to suitably 'stain' the brick paper where necessary, it is better to apply several thin coats rather than one heavy coat of paint, so that the final appearance can be built up gradually. Always keep a supply of clean cold water handy when carrying out this operation so that if a mistake is made it can be quickly washed away.

The roof of an old building is treated in a similar manner to the walls, but using the correct tile patterned paper instead of brick pattern. If heavy tiles are to be reproduced some form of 'relief modelling' is called for on the cardboard before the tile paper is applied. There are several ways of achieving this effect, the easiest being to make use of the fact that porous cardboard will distort if soaked in water and then subjected to quick drying in a heated atmosphere. Take the piece of cardboard to be used for the roof section in question and score it horizontally with the point of the Stanley knife held at an acute angle to the surface (see fig. 25). Next make cuts at right angles to these at the correct tile spacing, making sure that *alternating* course line up, and the cuts are not continuous, otherwise the roof will have the unrealistic appearance of a chess board. The piece of cardboard is next soaked for about twenty minutes, the time depending on the nature of the cardboard being used, tests will have to be carried out before the proper job is tackled. At the end of the soaking time, surplus water is shaken off and then the cardboard is immediately put near an open fire or in an oven for a few minutes. It will be seen that the individual 'tiles' have distorted sufficiently to resemble an uneven roof, and it may be possible to just paint them and not use tile patterned paper.

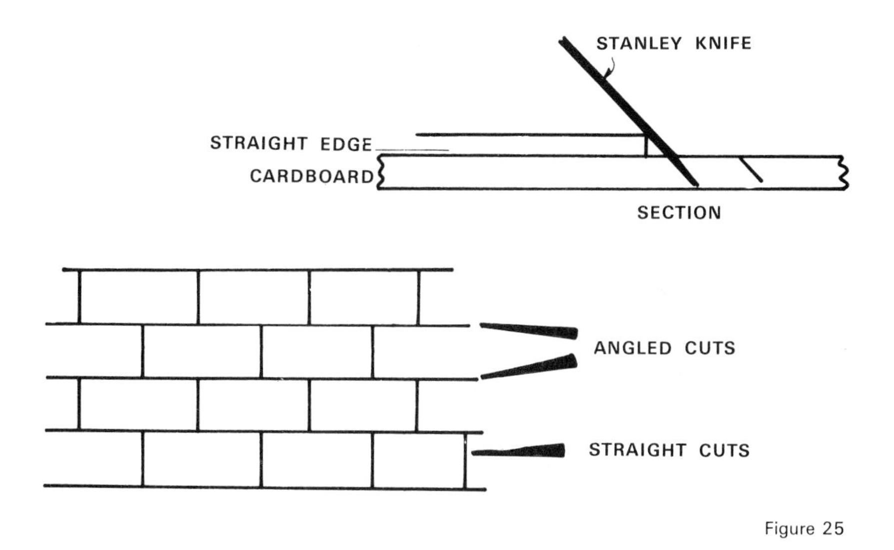

Figure 25

Trial and error is the only way to perfect this technique as there are so many variable factors to consider such as nature and thickness of cardboard, size of tiles created, soaking time, drying time and temperature, etc. After the main roof area is completed in this manner, any dormer windows or skylights appearing on the roof can be added, taking care that they follow the shape of the distorted roof.

If areas of lead are in evidence such as flashing or even complete leaded areas these can be fashioned from flattened out toothpaste tubes (and see p. 93), turned inside out of course, so that the lead-coloured inside is exposed to view.

Paved courtyards or cobbled areas surrounding old buildings are dealt with in a similar manner to the walls, namely by the use of several applications of glue and tissue paper before the correct patterned paper is fixed into place. Cobbled yards cannot show individual stones of course, but if an overall colour is achieved, then the cobble stones are indicated by quick dabs of undiluted Cryla colours at random over the surface.

When dealing with old buildings the windows present a particular problem as they are usually of different sizes and types. The ordinary casement window is easily dealt with by the use of drawn lines on celluloid or other transparent plastic material, but if lattice windows are to be made, it must be remembered that very rarely do they remain in a flat plane, usually they 'bulge' inwards where window cleaners or the weather have left their mark. One way of producing these windows is for the leaded sections to be made from copper wire, carefully soldered into the diamond or rectangular pattern usually adopted. Pieces of Sellotape are then taken and placed over the wire framework from both sides, so that the wire represents the filling in a sandwich. Further layers of Sellotape are built up from both sides until the window reaches the necessary thickness where it is strong enough to be trimmed to size for mounting in its framework. Before fitting into place however, it is necessary to draw lines on the outside following the wire shapes to give it the required grey 'lead' colour. When fitted into the building wall, it will be found that a very satisfactory bulge can be applied to the window by the application of a thumb or finger! Several layers of Sellotape also serve to give the appearance of obscure or old glass in the windows.

Many old buildings have stained glass windows, or sections of stained glass windows in them. If the building is small enough, a colour slide can be taken from inside the building, this can then be used instead of the normal celluloid, but usually the scale is not as convenient as that. The way to produce simulated stained glass windows, is to draw the window design out and then place a thin sheet of glass over the design. Sellotape is fixed to the glass covering the area of the drawing and sections to be 'stained' are cut out with a sharp knife point. These are replaced with coloured transparent paper which can be obtained from chocolate or toffee wrappings in many shades, fitted in like a jig-saw puzzle. After completion another piece of Sellotape is placed over the whole assembly and it is carefully peeled away from the glass base. It is now strong enough to be dealt with as a plain section of window would be, and can be incorporated into the framework or used as it is, depending on the size of the individual piece.

Chimneys on old buildings were usually quite complicated with protruding brickwork courses and inset panels in the sides of the chimney. These will present no problem, as they can be regarded simply as small buildings would be. Any recessed panels can be produced by cutting out an overlay of thin cardboard, and applying it to the chimney sides before fixing the brick-patterned paper into place, the edges of course being 'worn away' first to correspond to the rest of the building. The top of the chimney is built up in layers, the thickness of each layer corresponding to the thickness of brickwork in each layer (see fig. 26). Chimney pots were also very decorative in

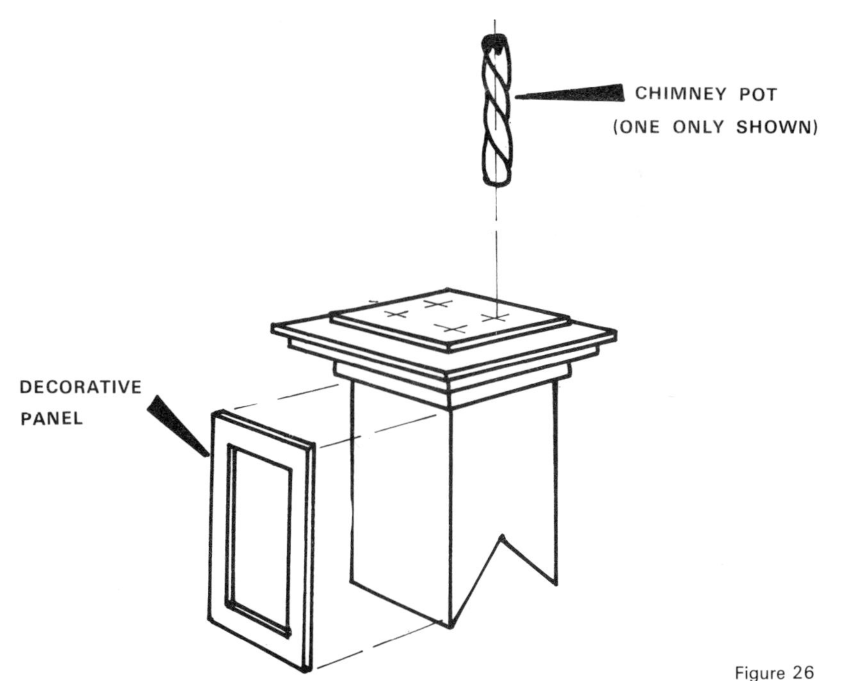

Figure 26

many instances, one type having a spiral shape moulded into the outside. A piece of suitable dowel rod is cut to length, glue and tissue paper are rolled on the outside of it, then it is taken gently between finger and thumb and 'twisted' evenly along its length before the glue has had time to dry. Any fancy shapes around the lip of the chimney pot are cut in with the Stanley knife, and the tops of the chimney pots are painted matt black. Some extra care should be taken in producing chimneys as models are usually viewed from above in the first instance and the chimneys are therefore the first part to be seen.

Life is given to old buildings on a model if the doors are shown in the half-open position with a figure or figures placed entering or leaving the building, and in some cases even the windows can be shown partly open. The only point which must be carefully watched out for, is that if windows are open then the interior framework of the model must not be visible through the open window, as there is a natural tendency for people to peer into the open windows! If there is a possibility that the interior construction details might be visible, it is advisable to paint the interior of the model near the open windows either matt black or dark grey.

Chapter X

Landscaping

The object of landscaping is to establish the model in its surroundings, the amount of actual landscaping being determined by the use for which the model is being made (illus. no. 18). It has previously been explained that the majority of the basic ground construction should take place before the buildings are set into position. We can now assume that the baseboard buildings and site surroundings are complete and the stage has been reached where 'life' is to be given to the model to complete it.

18. The flat roof looks most realistic when it is finished off with 'wet or dry' emery paper

Grassland

The first item, and probably the most important is the grassed areas constituting formal lawns, fields, golf course, banks, roadside verges, etc. It is possible to purchase ready mixed packets of dyed sawdust made up into various grades of grass such as 'coarse grass', 'buttercup field', 'lawn', etc. These are made for model railway enthusiasts to give realism to their layouts, and while they have a certain usefulness they do not give the serious model maker much scope for individual expression. If a supply of *fine* sawdust is obtained it can be loosely tied up in an old nylon stocking and dyed a medium green shade, following the dye manufacturer's instructions. A cold water dye is best and an old bucket should be used. After drying in a warm atmosphere this material forms the basis of all grassed areas, except putting greens, bowling greens or other very close-mown areas.

The method of application is to thickly paint the area to be grassed with any matt finish green paint, approximating to the shade of grass finally required, working on a small area at a time. The dyed sawdust is sprinkled fairly thickly over the paint and patted over lightly with a piece of sponge or soft foam rubber and then left until dry. This is most important otherwise bald patches may occur which are not easy to repair. The next operation is to turn the model upside down above a sheet of newspaper and lightly tap the base to release the surplus sawdust for future use. If the model is too heavy to hold upside down a soft artist's brush should be used instead to remove surplus sawdust. A thin mixture of paint can now be applied over the sawdust bringing it to the correct shade of green for the particular area. Remember that grass is never a uniform colour, as a change in colour and texture occurs around gateways, paths, etc. If a buttercup or daisy effect is required to emphasise the rough nature of a field, then light stippling with an old artist's brush cut off square at the top gives the necessary colour, but it should not be overdone otherwise realism is lost.

Where formal lawns or restricted areas of grass are required, the area should be masked off with strips of Sellotape clear tape or adhesive tape, which can be peeled off the baseboard after the grass has been completed, leaving a sharp edge to the area.

Bowling or putting greens follow a similar method, except that instead of sawdust, a fine flock mixture should be used in the correct light green colour as this cannot be painted over afterwards. If flock is used care should be taken as this is very light material and will float around a room for several hours settling onto furniture, etc., and can easily be *inhaled* by a careless model-maker!

Rocks and rocky outcrops

There are two or three basic methods of constructing rock formations, the particular method used depending on the scale of the model, and relative amount of rock detail to be incorporated.

19. A new office block with filling station surrounded by old buildings

On small scale models, cliffs and rocky ravines can be created by using cork bark, obtainable from florists. After fixing into place, the joints in the bark should be concealed by gluing cork chippings into place, then painting with matt paint roughly the same colour as the bark. This also applies where the bark joins the baseboard as no sharp edges should be visible. Sometimes difficulty is experienced in cutting cork bark with a plain knife and it will be found that a bread-saw or steak knife makes a better job of it. The natural rocky appearance is completed by dabs of green paint in corners and niches, to represent moss or grass tufts.

On larger scale models, cork bark is only used to represent rockeries or small rocky areas. Again, the joints should be concealed so that the rocks blend into the background. Where larger areas are to be shown on a model, use sheets of plaster-impregnated cotton gauze or hessian. This material is purchased very cheaply from furniture upholsterers, but sections of potato sacks are just as useful. With this method, balls of newspaper are rolled or screwed up, and glued into place here and there to give the required changes in height. A piece of hessian is next cut out larger than the area to be covered. Scotch glue is then heated up in a carpenter's glue-kettle, slightly thinner than normally required, and the hessian is immersed in it. After carefully spreading out the glued hessian over the newspaper balls (wearing rubber gloves to protect the hands) it is pinched into shape and allowed to set hard, after which it can be trimmed into shape, around the edges. If sufficient newspaper has been used it will be found that a solid, but lightweight base has been achieved, ready for painting into natural rocky colours.

Ploughed fields

On the smaller scale model these are represented by a plain brown area, but as the scale of the model increases individual furrows must be shown. The direction of the furrows normally follows the contours around the sides of hills, but orientation also plays a part in this. It is best to check with a local farmer before working on the model, just to be sure. The spacing of the furrows to the correct pitch, depending on scale, should be carefully calculated and noted. The area of the ploughed field is damped down, then covered with a thin layer of plaster of paris, or Cryla texture paste. When partly dry the furrows can be 'combed' in by using a piece of actual comb if the teeth spacing is correct, or alternatively panel pins can be knocked into a piece of scrap wood to the correct spacing and the heads removed. Remember that the furrows do not completely reach the edges of the field. All that now remains to be done is to paint the field in the correct earth colour, the shade depending on the locality, i.e. red clay, chalk, black soil, etc. The edges of the field are stippled green to represent grass, a final touch being tiny spots of bright red for poppies if they occur in the environment of the model.

Trees and bushes

A building development model, by its very nature, consists of hard cubes and straight lines in the main. To soften these lines and to set the buildings in their natural surroundings the careful use of trees is called for (see page 79). Many fine models are completely ruined by lack of attention to detail when producing trees, and this is often caused by lack of time as the model nears completion.

The basic material for the construction of deciduous trees such as oak, elm, hornbeam, etc., is natural sponge or artificial sponge. Natural sponge is best and old worn sponges can often be obtained from garages where they are no longer serviceable for washing cars—even quite small pieces have their uses.

Break the sponge into finger-nail size pieces, lightly tie them up in an old stocking, then dye them dark green. A good idea is to make up several small bundles so that they can be removed from the dye at different periods, thus giving a good selection of foliage material in different shades of green. At the same time a loofah should be purchased and cut into strips lengthwise, then dyed for the longest period. The loofah is useful for small bushes, hedges, climbing vines, window boxes and trailing plants, and has many other uses in this field. An examination of the construction of a loofah will reveal large cell pockets near the centre, with a closely packed fibrous outside. Pieces taken from the correct part of the loofah form a very lifelike representation of bushes, they can be touched lightly with blobs of paint to represent broom or gorse bushes, and various types of flowering shrub. When thoroughly dried out, the sponge pieces should be stored in open trays, graded according to the depth of colour, where they are immediately to hand for the construction of trees.

There are several children's books on the market dealing with the subject of tree identification; it will be observed that trees vary depending on type, height relative to width or diameter, compactness of foliage, depth of colour, etc.

The method of construction for most deciduous trees is the same, but it is most important that the final size of tree relative to the particular model and scale should be closely watched, as it is very easy to make the trees out of scale, thus completely destroying the lifelike appearance of the model. A good supply of electric wire should be obtained, the most useful grade being wire used for the installation of electric cookers or power mains in houses. This should be stripped of its covering and insulation leaving sections of bare wire which should be cut into lengths of about 6″ for ease of working. Six or eight strands of the wire should be twisted together for the estimated length of the trunk up to the fork of the tree, plus an allowance for fitting into the baseboard (see fig. 27). Three or four strands are pulled away from the outer edge at this height to form the outer branches of the tree, the remaining wires being twisted together to the height of the secondary forks, from which position they are splayed out to complete the shape of the tree.

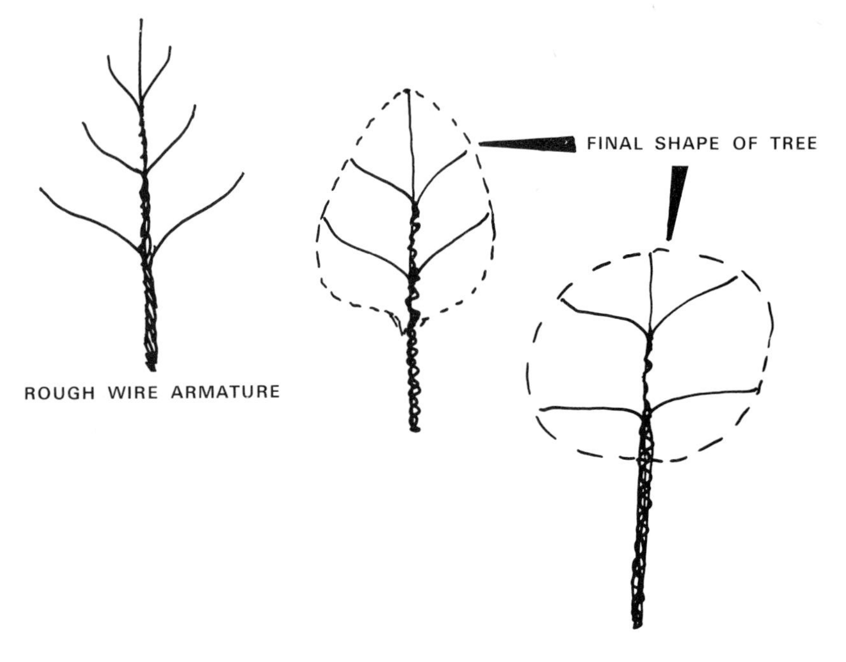

Figure 27

At this stage the framework can be painted using Cryla colours or matt paint. Some brown and grey paint should be made available, a dab of each following the line of the trunk and branches, finishing off with streaks of white give a very realistic bark effect, the balance of colours being determined by the type of tree being modelled. When thoroughly dry, the sponge can be glued on to the wire frame in small pieces, leaving spaces in between otherwise the final effect is lost. The sponge at the centre and north side of the trees can be slightly darker than the outer edge and south side to give 'modelling' to the tree together with greater realism. If near the coast, remember that the tendency is for trees to lean away from the sea and the foliage itself is often out of balance.

Conifers are very easy to make, since they usually consist of a straight trunk with branches in clearly defined layers. There are many kinds of nylon 'bottle brushes' which can be pressed into service for the manufacture of this type of tree. Electric razor cleaning brushes, test-tube brushes, centres of ladies' hair rollers, these are all vital to the model maker and only require trimming and painting.

There are cases where ornamental flowering blossom trees are required along a driveway or approach to a hotel, or as an ornamental garden attached to a public building. These are usually quite small compared to mature trees, and in any case are much more delicate in appearance if made as young trees. Make a wire armature as for other trees, but with the branches much shorter, only three or four wires might be required. After painting the wire framework or armature it is dipped in liquid glue, or glue is brushed on to the branches, after which it is liberally sprinkled with cork chippings and allowed to dry. The cork chippings are then roughly brushed with dark green paint as a base for the 'blossom' and the greater part of the cork chippings are painted in a combination of pink and white or red and white depending on the type of blossom represented. After fixing into place on the baseboard a final touch is to secure a cocktail stick as a stake with fuse wire and to paint a few 'fallen blossoms' on the ground immediately at the foot of the tree. This effect should be used sparingly, a mere suggestion of fallen blossoms is sufficient to create the illusion.

Tamarisk bushes can be represented by using coarse steel wool for foliage, attached to the wire armature then dipped into brownish-pink paint and shaken in a plastic bag to remove the surplus paint, after which the leaves and branches can be suggested by a few strokes of brown paint.

On small scale models wire armatures are not necessary for bushes and small trees. A panel pin driven partly into the baseboard, painted brown and the sponge attached is all that is required to give a good representation of a tree.

20. Housing estate. The mature trees existing on the site are faithfully reproduced

Rivers, lakes and seashore

Very few architectural models are produced that do not have some stretches of water in them. Small scale models may have a river or seashore as an integral part of the model, larger scale models may have ornamental ponds or lakes.

Rivers can be constructed by several methods, and some experiments should be carried out to determine the best for a particular situation. Unlike a pond or lake, a river seldom has clear water as it is usually flowing along carrying mud with it. It is a mistake therefore to show a river on a model as being crystal clear. One method of constructing a river is to cut away a depression in the baseboard (fig. 28) and line it with cooking foil (crumpled is just as effective as new). Above the foil is placed a sheet of transparent

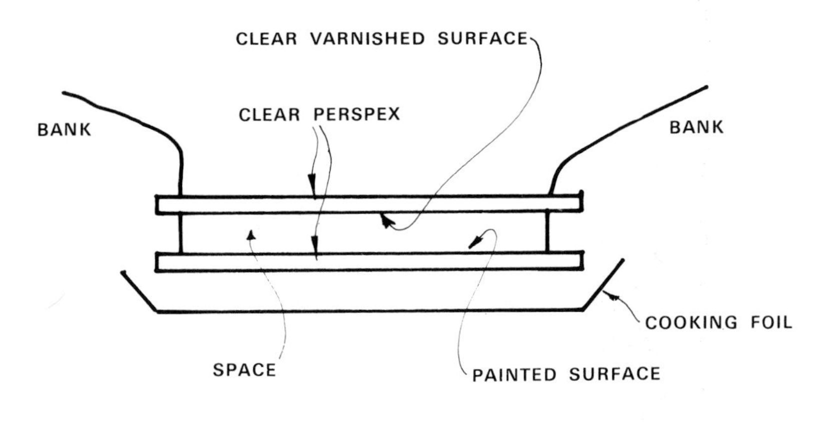

Figure 28

plastic or celluloid which is painted deep blue/green at the centre, gradually lighter towards the edges, with the outer edges brown or sandy-coloured depending on the locality. The paint should be applied in bold strokes with a few clear streaks left for the cooking foil to reflect through. Above the painted celluloid a small gap is left and the surface of the river is completed by a strip of 'rippled' pattern glass as used in bathrooms, or clear celluloid or plastic can be employed, varnished in long bold strokes on the underside. The object of this method is for the light to be reflected from the foil surface up through the 'water' as the viewer moves around the model, creating quite a natural appearance. Deep ponds and lakes can also be made this way;

a greater impression of depth is created if the cooking foil is not included so that the only reflection possible is from the top surface. Swimming pools or ornamental ponds call for a similar technique except that the colours used do not include any brown, a light blue/green colour only being used.

On a small-scale model the river or lake can be painted directly on to the excavated surface, 'ripple' glass or clear plastic then being placed in direct contact with the painted surface. It is most important that the edges of the glass or plastic are softened by banks, etc., otherwise a most unnatural appearance results.

If the seashore is to be included in a small scale model, this is usually along one edge, and can easily be created by chamfering away the baseboard as in fig. 29. The degree of cutting away is determined by

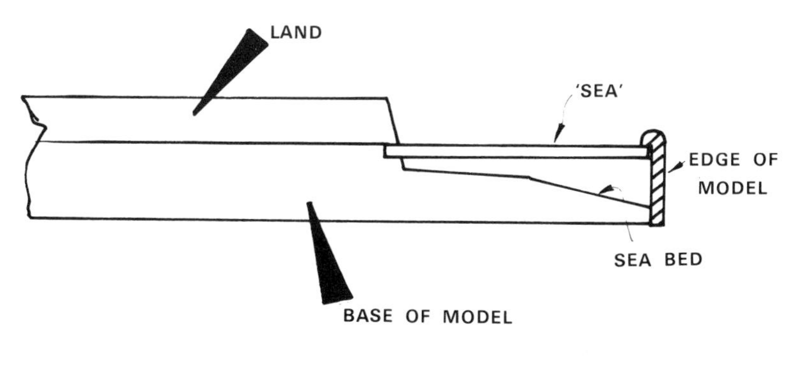

Figure 29

the rate with which the sea-bed falls away, if it gently 'shelves' then the sea-bed is only shown in a light sand colour. Actual sand can be used sprinkled on to the wet paint if an even more realistic effect is required. It might be necessary to indicate sections of sea-weed covered rocks that will be exposed at low tide, as the rocks will be covered by the glass or perspex surface of the sea it is quite in order to use pieces of modelling clay to form the rocks.

Wire fences and grill floors

The firms that make sheets of transfer letters also supply sheets of 'tone' for filling in larger areas on drawings, or in printers' blockmaking. Some of these, in black or white, can be fixed to thin transparent plastic sheets to form 'chain link' fencing, but care must

be taken to select the correct grid pattern for the scale being used. A larger grid pattern can be cut into sections and transferred directly to the baseboard for the grill floors to car-wash buildings or manhole covers.

Pieces of parallel-lined 'tone' sheets, when attached to clear plastic give a very good impression of iron railings, as the clear plastic is not apparent when fixed to the model. New patterns are being introduced all the time and the thoughtful model-maker will watch out for these and carry out experiments to improve his technique and the quality of the models produced.

Scaled accessories

Models gain in appearance by the addition of 'Trafficast' scale accessories (see page 84). Scale road vehicles, human figures, railway rolling stock, street furniture, boats and other outdoor items instantly add interest, realism and a sense of scale to the model. The use of 'Trafficast' scale toilet fittings, furniture and human figures in interior modelling will result in a much greater realism. The range has been specially produced for use in architectural model-making in a wide selection of the most frequently used scales. Vehicles are made in soft alloy, plastic or super-hard plaster, depending on size and type of vehicle. All vehicles have integrally cast fixing pegs, which can easily be snipped off if the model is free-standing. Human figures are produced generally in soft alloy. The limbs of figures to $\frac{1}{16}''$ scale and larger scales can be bent into various postures. This should be done before applying any paint. All figures have integrally cast fixing pegs.

All models are offered painted or unpainted. Painted vehicles are finished in semi-gloss paint with sufficient detail to express the character of the item. Painted figures are matt. Most of the items are supplied from stock; a general idea of the scales and range of products available is set out in the chart for guidance (see fig. 47), but a very comprehensive catalogue is published by the manufacturers, whose address is given in the Acknowledgements.

Opposite:

21. Rocks and trees fit naturally into the landscape

Scaled accessories

	1:1250 ($\frac{1}{100}''$)	1:1000 ($\frac{1}{88}''$)	1:800 ($\frac{1}{66}''$)	1:500 ($\frac{1}{40}''$ & $\frac{1}{44}''$)	1:400 ($\frac{1}{30}''$ & $\frac{1}{32}''$)	1:250 ($\frac{1}{20}''$, $\frac{1}{22}''$ & $\frac{1}{24}''$)	1:200 ($\frac{1}{16}''$)	1:150 ($\frac{1}{12}''$)	1:100 ($\frac{1}{8}''$)	1:50 ($\frac{1}{4}''$)	1:25 ($\frac{1}{2}''$)	1:12 (1″)
Car	●	●	●	●	●	●	●	●	●			
Taxi			●	●	●		●					
Ambulance	●	●	●	●	●		●		●			
Land Rover				●	●		●					
Light lorry (open)		●	●	●	●		●		●			
Light lorry (box)				●			●		●			
Medium lorry (open)				●	●	●	●	●	●			
Medium lorry (load)							●					
Medium lorry (box)				●	●	●	●		●			
Medium tanker							●					
Removal van	●	●	●	●	●	●	●		●			
Heavy lorry (open)				●	●	●	●					
Heavy lorry (load)	●	●	●	●	●	●	●					
Heavy lorry (low)							●					
Heavy lorry (high)							●					
Road tanker	●	●	●	●	●	●	●		●			
Artic. lorry (open)					●		●					
Artic. lorry (load)							●					
Artic. lorry (box)					●		●		●			
Artic. tanker					●		●		●			
Coach			●	●	●		●	●				
Single deck bus	●	●	●	●	●	●	●					
Double deck bus	●	●	●	●	●	●	●	●	●			
Trailer (open)				●	●		●					
Trailer (box)				●	●		●					
Trailer (tanker)					●		●					
Refuse lorry				●			●					
Transit mixer				●			●					
Airport tractor							●					
Airport trailer							●					
Fork lift truck							●					
Lamp post (coolie hat)						●	●		●			
Light standard (DBL)				●	●	●	●		●			
Light standard (SIN)				●	●	●	●		●			
Dust bin							●					
Phone box							●					
Police box							●					

Scaled accessories

	1 : 1250 ($\frac{1}{100}''$)	1 : 1000 ($\frac{1}{88}''$)	1 : 800 ($\frac{1}{66}''$)	1 : 500 ($\frac{1}{40}''$ & $\frac{1}{44}''$)	1 : 400 ($\frac{1}{30}''$ & $\frac{1}{32}''$)	1 : 250 ($\frac{1}{20}''$, $\frac{1}{22}''$ & $\frac{1}{24}''$)	1 : 200 ($\frac{1}{16}''$)	1 : 150 ($\frac{1}{12}''$)	1 : 100 ($\frac{1}{8}''$)	1 : 50 ($\frac{1}{4}''$)	1 : 25 ($\frac{1}{2}''$)	1 : 12 ($1''$)
Pillar box							●					
Traffic obelisk							●					
Traffic signal (DBL)							●					
Traffic signal (SIN)							●					
Toilet fittings									●	●	●	
Outdoor male				●	●	●	●	●	●	●	●	●
Outdoor female				●	●	●	●	●	●	●	●	●
Indoor male							●		●	●		
Indoor female							●		●	●		
Male child							●		●	●		
Female child							●		●	●		
Male youth							●					
Sitting male							●		●	●		
Sitting female							●		●	●		
Perambulator							●					
Domestic furniture									●			
Goods truck	●			●			●					
Box wagon	●			●			●					
Oil tanker	●			●			●					
Passenger coach	●			●			●					
Shunting loco.				●			●					
Main line loco.	●			●			●					
Guards van				●			●					
Dockside crane	●											
Dinghy				●								
Yacht				●	●							
Catamaran				●								
Cabin cruiser				●	●							
Barge				●	●							
Tug				●	●							
Cows				●								
Sheep				●								

Chapter XI

Found objects

'Found Objects' is a term used by artists to indicate materials in a collage which are normally scrap, but which the artist can use in his work. Several examples in art galleries show items such as buttons, torn newspapers, bus tickets and pieces of driftwood forming works of art by Picasso and others, indicating that to the discerning eye there is no such thing as 'rubbish'. The model-maker should develop this outlook, and gather together several boxes of miscellaneous materials, roughly divided into wood, plastic, card and paper, wire and metal, etc. As experience is gained in the use of these materials ingenious uses will be found for all sorts of discarded items. Here are some of the more obvious ones:

Ball-point pen refills

These should always be cleaned out when exhausted by carefully passing through them a pipe cleaner which has been dipped in the special solvent supplied for removing ball-point pen stains from fingers or clothing. When clean they should be divided into appropriate sizes, as different makes of ball-point pens have refill tubes of different diameters.

A method of constructing 'stick-lights' on garage models has already been described (fig. 19, p. 54), but these sections of plastic tubing also have a place in the construction of street lamps. First of all a fine hole is drilled in the base board and a length of welding rod or bicycle spoke is tapped into place. Next a piece of refill tubing is slipped over the rod and attached to the baseboard with a spot of clear Bostik. The head of the lamp is bent over to the correct angle, depending on the design, and another piece of tubing is glued into place for the light (see fig. 30). The lamp standard is painted grey, leaving a small fillet of paint above the tubing at the base; the lamp is completed by painting the light itself white.

Sections of the tubing can be glued side by side on a roof to form 'Spanish tiles' if the model is of a scale where this effect is required.

Owing to its flexible nature, it can also be used for handrails to

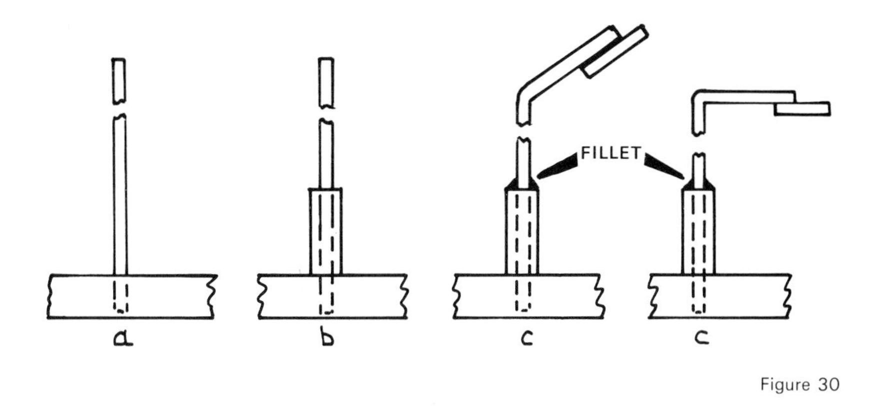

Figure 30

spiral staircases, or other curved staircases. The method used is to tap in panel pins for the handrail supports. Fine holes to take the supports can be inserted in the tubing by holding a panel pin or length of wire in pliers, heating it up in a spirit lamp flame, and then piercing the tubing with it through to the centre. A dab of clear Bostik will secure the handrail in place.

Box cameras

Old box cameras can be broken down to yield a wonderful supply of material. The shutter mechanism itself usually contains fine springs and levers which can be used in models where a certain amount of operation is required such as the closure of panels concealing miniature light switches. The viewfinder consists of a piece of glass rectangular in shape, convex on both sides. When inserted into the roof above a staircase well in a model of an office or flat development, it becomes a roof-light approximately 4′ 0″ long and 3′ 0″ wide if the scale of the model is 1″ to 8′ 0″. If an interior model of a building is being fitted out with miniature furniture, then it is a television screen to a scale of $\frac{1}{4}$″ to 1″! Many other uses will occur to the model maker when this item has been handled a few times. The actual lens of the camera is useful for concealed lighting fittings in model shops, the effect is enhanced considerably when miniature bulbs are placed behind it and lit up, but more of this in the section dealing with the lighting of models. The hinged back of a box camera is worth keeping, as the hinge itself is finely constructed and has many uses as such. The thin metal sections usually surrounding the film chamber can be cut into strips with metal shears to form useful fine brackets for holding shop fronts or fascias into place on buildings, or kept in flat sections to give hidden strength to a model where cardboard or balsa wood would receive undue strain.

Buttons and badges

Buttons of unusual shapes should be kept, particularly if they are embossed or engraved in any way. On a small scale model of a modern building they form a good piece of sculpture above an entrance door, or relief wall mural at the end of a corridor. Ordinary buttons of various sizes make good ornamental concrete flower tubs in models of shopping precints or outside public buildings. They should be painted a white matt finish, small tufts of wool pulled out of carpet samples provide the foliage, and dabs of bright red Cryla paint or sealing wax complete the construction by adding the flowers. Badges are mostly die-cast and sometimes consist of a manufacturer's name or trademark. They can be fixed to shop fronts as the name-plate, or used to represent neon signs on small scale buildings. The pressed type of badge can have the pin removed and be used for 'dome-lights' on the roof of an office block or flats.

Cotton

After constructing pylons and crane gantries from strip wood, cotton can be passed back and forth between the uprights to represent bracing wires or ties. They should be glued at their intersections, and painted for added strength.

If agricultural buildings are to be incorporated in a model, it is usual for stables or cattle sheds to be in evidence. The floor of these buildings is invariably littered with straw or hay, in addition to which bales of hay are in the mangers. Yellow embroidery cotton is useful to represent this, it is necessary to cut it into $\frac{1}{4}''$ or $\frac{1}{2}''$ lengths and dip it into thinned down glue or gum before fixing into place. Do not attempt to cut the cotton a strand at a time, otherwise you will take many hours over this job alone! Take several skeins of cotton and bind them tightly together, cutting straight through the bunch with a sharp razor blade or Stanley knife. If bales of hay are to be manufactured, use yellow or brown modelling clay for the main shape, dip it into glue and attach two or three layers of cotton lengths to the outside. When scattering the 'straw' on the floor of a building, after it has been dipped in the glue, lightly press it into place with a piece of foam rubber, then it should be lightly sprayed with an aerosol fixative, as used for transfer lettering or charcoal.

Christmas cards and leaflets

All christmas cards, birthday cards and manufacturers' leaflets with coloured designs and unbroken coloured areas should be saved, as these can be used for interior finishes to model buildings. When cut to size they can cover counter tops, table tops, small walls or alcoves, sometimes even act as abstract or modern paintings in an office or house interior. Manufacturers' catalogues usually show a photographed facsimile of the product, and if this happens to be wood-grain panelling or tiling, its usefulness is at once apparent!

Paint shade cards

Most painting contractors have a few obsolete 'trade shade cards' or they can be obtained from the paint manufacturers direct. A section of the appropriate coloured card fixed behind a cut-out doorway to a model building immediately produces the correctly coloured door with a finish superior in every way to a hand painted one (see fig. 31).

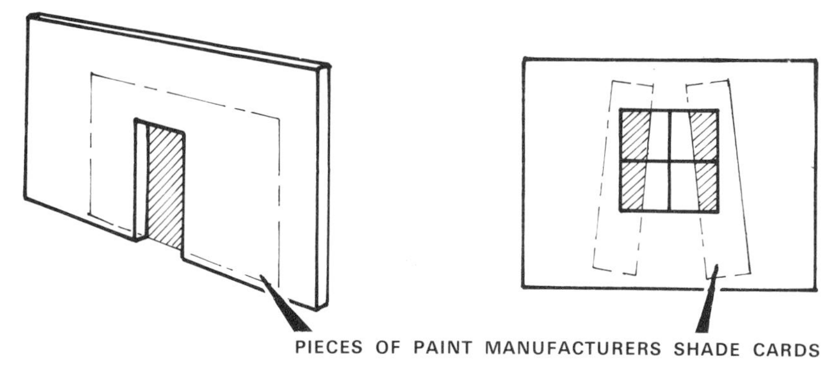

Figure 31

When a thin strip of the card is attached behind the clear perspex or celluloid forming a window, from the outside this gives a good representation of curtains or blinds, depending on which way it is fixed. It is not necessary to cut out the pieces with great accuracy, as most of the card is not seen from the outside of the building.

Pipe cleaners

On very small scale models, short sections of pipe cleaner glued into a drilled hole in the baseboard give a very good representation of evergreen trees, when painted dark green. If they are fixed in regular rows with 'fire breaks' left between areas, a forest can be created at little cost and trouble.

One of the best uses for pipe cleaners is to make the revolving brushes seen on automatic car washes in most modern garages, a study of the manufacturer's catalogue will show that most car washes are constructed on a similar principle. The model maker can simplify the construction if he thinks of an arch of square or rectangular section carrying the brushes, the complete assembly running on rails.

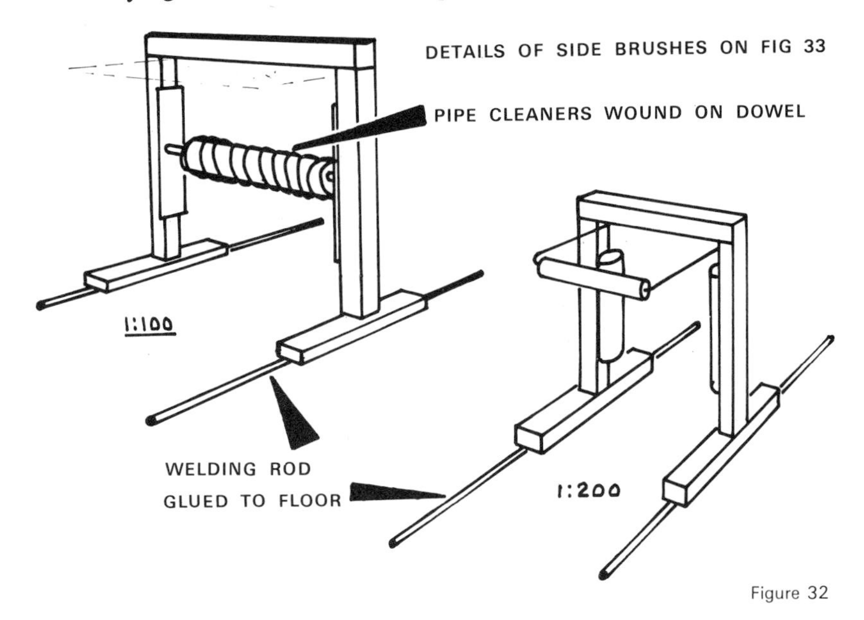

Figure 32

Sections of pipe cleaner are used, cut to length, for models of $\frac{1}{16}'' = 1'\ 0''$ or 1 to 200 (see fig. 32), but in a larger scale such as $\frac{1}{8}'' = 1'\ 0''$ or 1 to 100, then it becomes necessary to wind sections of pipe cleaners around a section of fine wooden dowel to represent brushes. The horizontal brush in the smaller scale model is a piece of pipe cleaner with the 'fluff' scraped off from each end, and the wire bent at right angles to enable the brush to stick out from the arch. In the larger scale model however, the pipe cleaner is wound around the rod, this is then glued firmly between the uprights of the arch. The vertical brushes are either glued directly onto the uprights of the arch in the smaller scale model, or attached to a piece of thin cardboard which in turn is fixed to the arch in the larger model (see fig. 33).

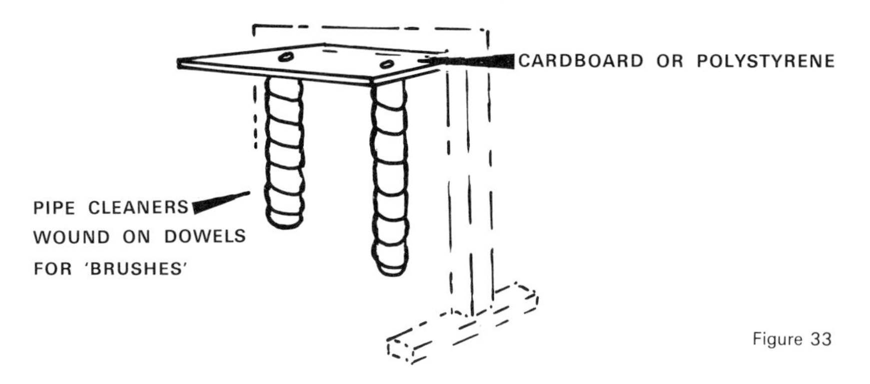

Figure 33

Plastic mesh

In these days of plastics, it is possible to obtain pieces of perforated nylon or plastic from flour sieves, filters of various kinds, plastic shopping bags, boxes, trays, toys, etc. All sections of plastic mesh thus obtained should be kept aside, as many uses for them will occur as a model progresses. Fine mesh can be cut into strips for gratings or industrial stair treads, for iron fire escapes or iron grid 'mezzanine' floors in an engineering works, or screens across ventilator shafts. Larger mesh pieces make good ornamental screen walls on a housing development model, cut into strips it is also possible to use it for barrier rails at busy road junctions, or protective barriers along the edges of flat roofs on apartment blocks or office blocks.

Plastic hair rollers

The type of plastic hair roller most useful to the model maker is the cylindrical kind with an insert similar to a bottle brush. These are used extensively by hairdressers, and as they are comparatively cheap they are usually discarded in quantity. The exterior of the hair roller consists of a coarse flexible mesh material, the mesh is square or rectangular in section and being flexible can be bent into any shape after being cut into sections. Many ways of using it will become apparent, the most obvious being for ladders, barriers, staircases and fencing.

The 'bottle brush' interiors of the hair rollers make excellent evergreen trees 20′ to 25′ high if the model is 1 to 100 scale. They should be lightly singed with a candle to partly dissolve the nylon bristles, then dipped into dark green paint and shaken in a plastic bag to get rid of the surplus paint (fig. 34). If the tree is required to be tapered, this can be done with a Stanley knife or sharp scissors prior to painting. The lower $\frac{1}{4}''$ or so of the 'stem' should be scraped clear of all bristles and painted brown before fixing into a hole in the base.

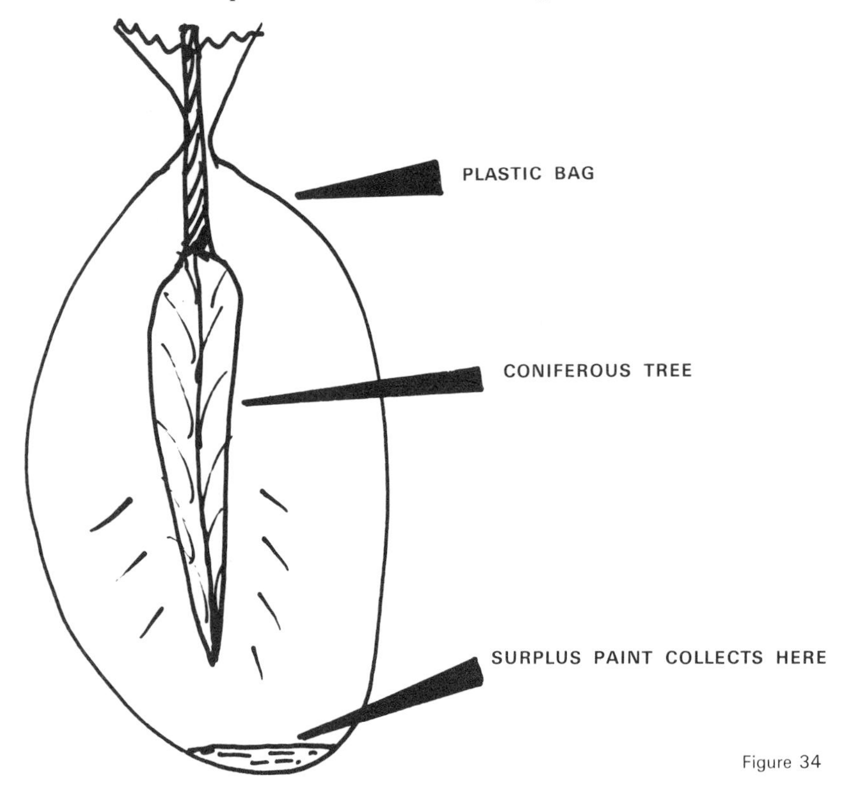

Figure 34

Tooth-paste tubes

The large size should be saved, the top and 'neck' removed, and the tube opened out by slitting along the seam, or one side. After thoroughly cleaning in hot soapy water and drying, the tube can be made into a flat smooth sheet of metal by rubbing it with the back of an old spoon, against a hard surface such as a table top or working bench.

One of the most versatile ways in which this material can be used is in the production of sculptural wall murals, low relief 'carvings', plaques, coats-of-arms, and other decorative features (see illus. 16).

22. Multi-storey office block with an ornamental pond forming an important part of the scheme

The method of working is to take a thick pile of newspapers, or tissue paper, and place the piece of flattened metal on to it, with the unpainted side down. The design to be produced is now drawn on the painted side of the metal sheet, i.e., the original outside of the tooth-paste tube, then gone over lightly with a fine ball-point pen or blunt scriber point, care being taken not to puncture the metal. It may be necessary to trace over the design several times to obtain the required 'relief', but when the piece of soft metal is removed from the pad of newspaper, it will be observed that the design is outstanding. This only requires trimming to size with scissors before gluing into place on the model building. If left in its natural state a 'lead' appearance is produced, but the finished item will look very realistic when painted in its correct colours.

Flattened out tooth-paste tubes can also be used for making small sections of rain-water guttering, 'lead' roof covering to outhouses, or small buildings, or for lead flashing to chimneys. Thin sections of it rolled and twisted will produce all sorts of interesting shapes for wrought ironwork, in fact the keen model maker will spend a long time experimenting with this very cheap but useful material.

Plastic 'bubbles'

Nowadays many items sold in shops are mounted on cards for display and ease of handling. These cards usually have the merchandise contained within transparent plastic 'bubbles' so that it is visible to the prospective purchaser. When the transparent plastic is removed from the card it immediately becomes of great use to the model maker, because some of the shapes produced by the moulding process cannot readily be duplicated by the amateur. All shapes can be saved, as only small pieces of each will be used for domes, curved windows, etc. In certain instances these transparent mouldings can be let into the outside wall of a building to give a glimpse of the interior, without giving an impression that it is a natural window. The sort of goods usually fixed to this type of card include tooth-brushes, shoe brushes, small tools, motorists' accessories, photographic items, toys, etc.

Chapter XII

Lighting

Generally speaking, an architectural model is viewed under natural daylight conditions, or artificial room lighting. There are, however, instances when a feature of the development being modelled is the 'night time' appearance of the new buildings in relation to their surroundings. A typical case is the construction of a 24-hour service garage with an illuminated canopy above the petrol pumps, in this instance the surrounding houses should be constructed normally, but the area to be occupied by the garage should be cut out completely from the baseboard and treated as a separate unit. The petrol pumps, cars and figures should be attached in their natural position on the cut out section, but as it will be necessary to remove the majority of the $\frac{1}{2}''$ thick chipboard from the cut out piece, the positioning of the cars and figures is critical (see fig. 35).

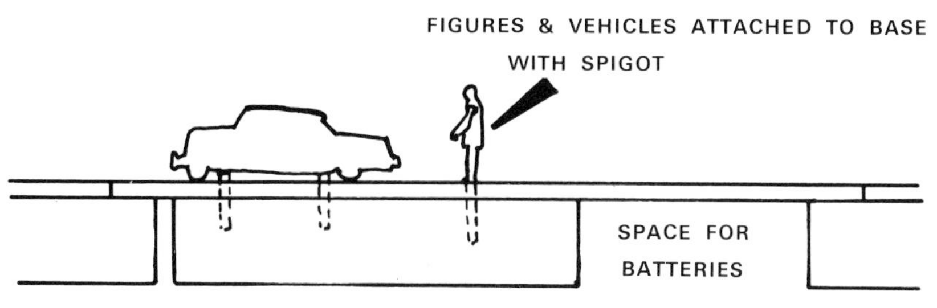

Figure 35

The property of perspex to transmit light is next brought into use. It will be necessary to drill two holes in the perspex to accept the two tiny 4-volt bulbs which will be used in the lighting scheme, with sufficient clearance around them to allow a small air cavity for cooling. The tiny bulbs have thin twin wires attached to them, and they are sold as part of a dolls house furniture range. The holes in the perspex should be clear of the positions where the effect of strip lighting is required, and close enough to the tubular supporting columns for the wiring to have a short run (see fig. 36).

The top of the canopy is covered with foil to give maximum reflection through the underside of the perspex, then topped off with wet and dry paper to give the finished effect to the canopy. The underside

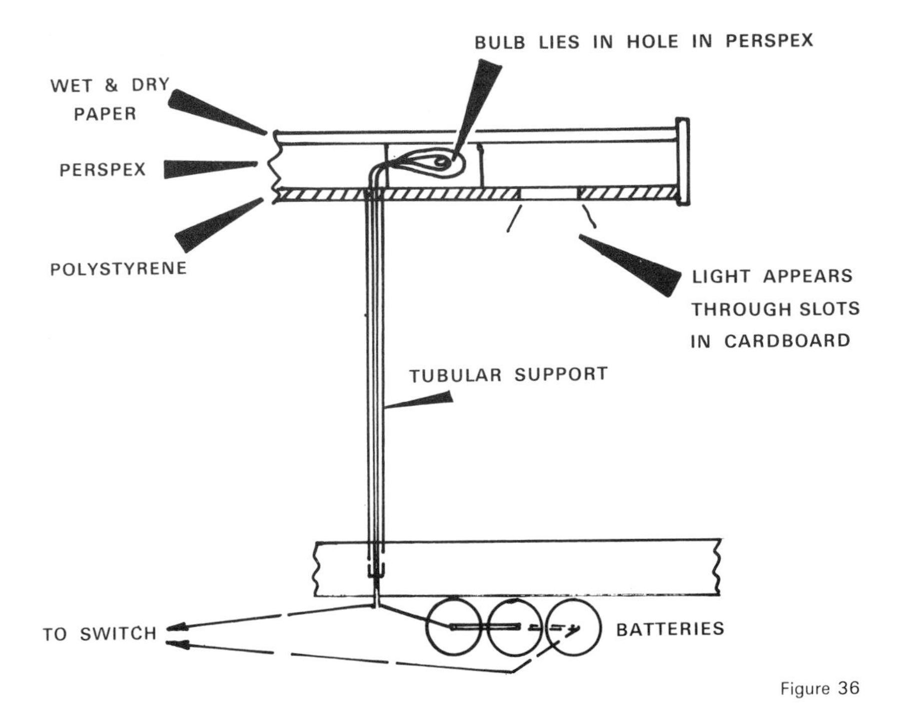

Figure 36

of the perspex is covered with white card or white polystyrene sheet, except for the 'strip lighting' sections, where a thin strip of clear perspex or acrylic is inserted. It is necessary to use thin tubing for the supporting columns as the wires have to be carried through to the underside of the baseboard.

Having finished the canopy, and other 'above ground' items, the power supply can be installed. This consists of three hearing-aid batteries, or pencil torch batteries each of $1\frac{1}{2}$ volts connected end to end to give the necessary power to the two bulbs. It is hardly necessary to state that the 4 volt bulbs are wired in 'parallel', they would only receive 2 volts each if wired in 'series'. A simple brass contact is made across the ends of the batteries, and a connection made to a switch in a neutral area of the model. When the switch is operated the canopy will throw a good light in a downwards direction where the clear sections have been left, giving an extremely realistic impression of fluorescent lighting strips. It should be stressed that the lights should only be operated for short periods due to the problems of overheating in the confined apertures where the bulbs are located, and the difficulty of replacing bulbs when they burn out.

A similar effect can be obtained by constructing 'stick lights' from perspex rod and installing a small light in the baseboard to transmit its light through the rod giving an illuminated effect only through the unpainted sections. Perspex rod can be bent easily in boiling water or over a flame as the light will 'bend' with it, this property of the material will be used by the inventive model maker to produce 'porthole' lights in shop fronts and similar applications (see fig. 37). Several lights can be produced from the same bulb, as the light will travel in any direction, provided a piece of perspex rod is there to guide it around the corners!

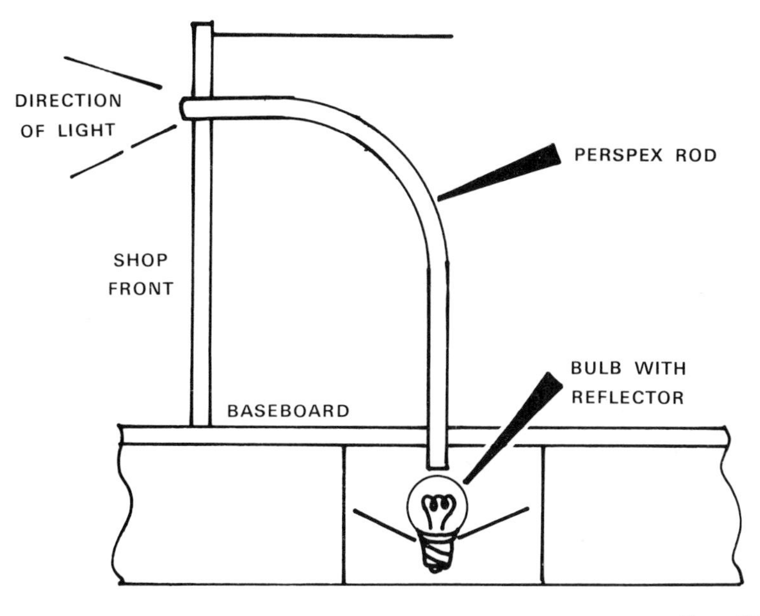

Figure 37

It should be emphasised that all interior lighting should be carried out with low voltage lighting using dry batteries wherever possible, all wiring should be properly insulated and of the correct thickness or gauge for the voltage used. An alternative to batteries is a mains transformer with an output of up to 12 volts, but *direct mains should never be used under any circumstances.*

There are instances where it is necessary to produce houses or other buildings internally lit for certain special effects. This is quite easy to do, the basic method of construction needs to be modified slightly to prevent unwanted shadows, and generally speaking the houses so lit will be capable of being removed from the baseboard. When the baseboard and landscaping have been completed, a bulb and bulbholder are mounted in the centre of each house location, and connected up beneath the baseboard to the switch and batteries, in 'series' or 'parallel' depending on the numbers of illuminated positions to be installed, and the numbers and locations of batteries employed.

The houses are constructed with a large hole in the base, big enough to fit over the bulb holder with adequate clearance, and the internal bracing sections of the house must run *diagonally* with a semicircle cut into the bottom to clear the bulb (see fig. 38). The windows in each wall of the house will then receive an uninterrupted amount of light from the bulb, at the same time the 'hollow' appearance of the house is not seen due to the appearance of the diagonal baffle walls. The houses are glued to the base at corners only, so that they can be removed to replace bulbs.

When illuminated shop fronts are required, a very effective method is to produce the name on a sheet of cardboard using Letraset transfer lettering. This is photographed, producing a negative the correct size required for the shop front name. Although comparatively expensive

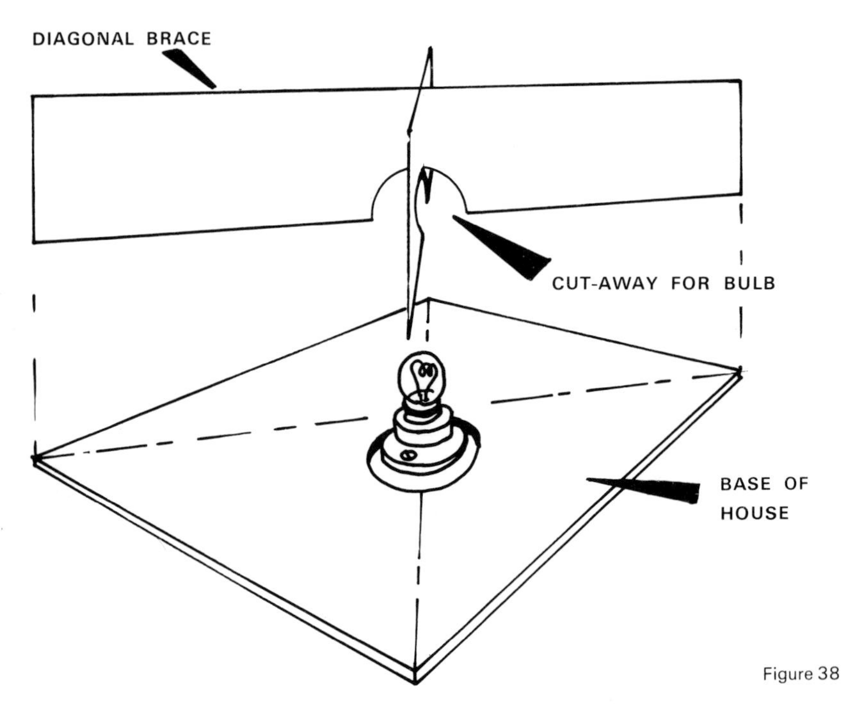

Figure 38

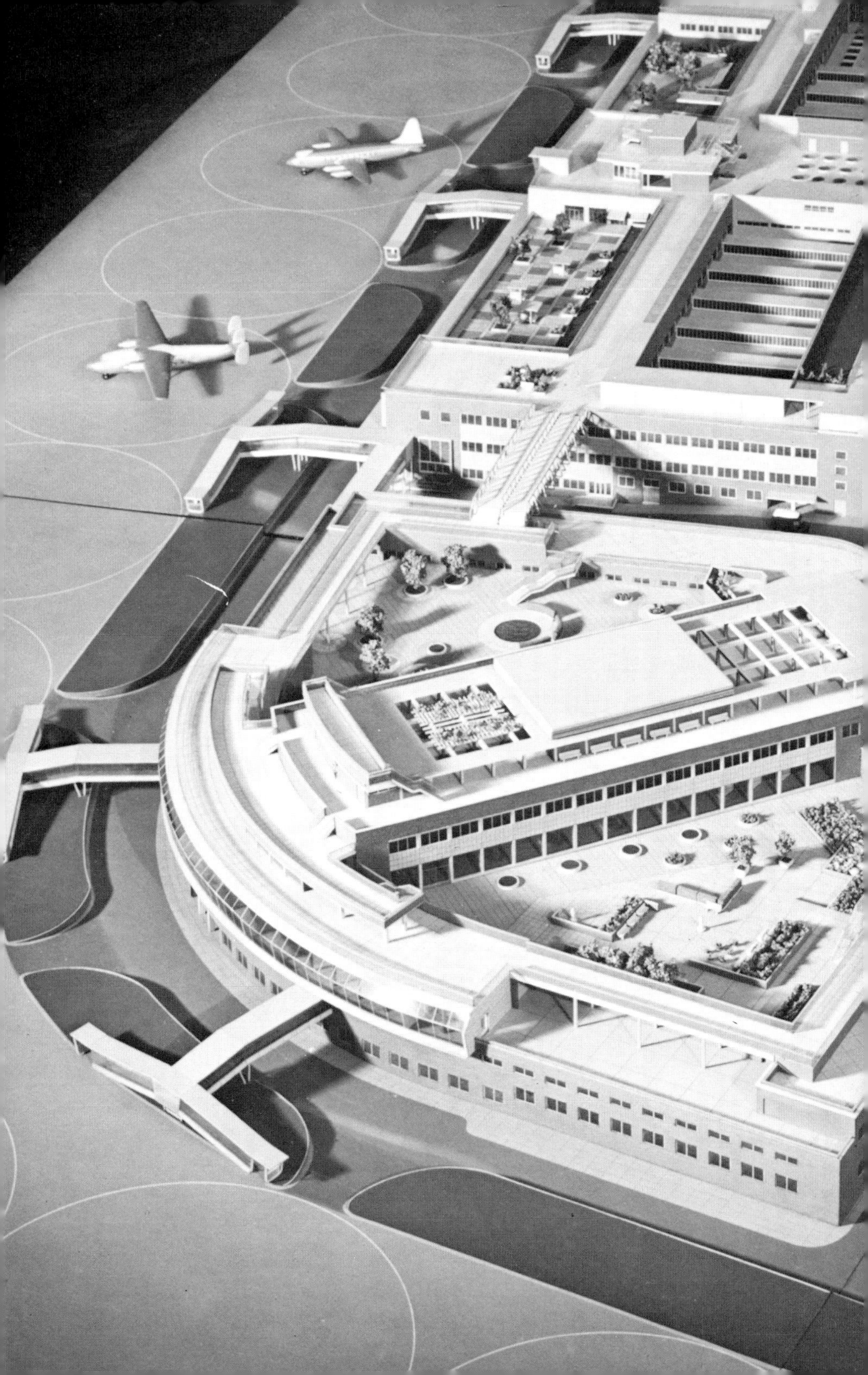

for the amateur model maker to produce it is far more effective and quicker to make than trying to cut out the individual letters by hand. The negative is backed up by a piece of suitably coloured cellophane or thin acrylic sheet, and illuminated from the rear taking care that the light source is indirect, and no bulb filaments are visible through the transparent letters.

On previous page:
23. Municipal airport model

Chapter XIII

Display and storage

When a model has been completed, the method of displaying and storing it is determined by the original use for which the model was constructed. If it was made as a simple exercise to study form and space, then it is only necessary to place it in a box or plastic bag and put it away for future reference.

The majority of models covered by the preceding chapters, however, will be quite bulky, most bases being 2′ 0″ to 3′ 0″ square, the overall height of the models will be 4″ to 6″ and liable to suffer damage if handled carelessly. It is possible to obtain large plastic bags which can be slipped over the model to keep dust away, these are sold as dustbin liners or dress covers for use in wardrobes, and they are very cheap. Their use is limited to storage and transportation only, and a model should never be displayed or shown to a client or 'viewing' audience whilst still in its cover.

If the model is going to be on view for a short time, such as during a planning committee meeting, then it is necessary for the model maker to arrive at the display room about an hour before the committee meets. This will give him time to remove the plastic covering carefully, arrange the model to advantage, make the best use of the available lighting, and ensure that it is placed where it will not suffer undue damage or handling.

The only time it is necessary to display a model in a glass case, or one made from transparent perspex, is when the model in question is to be on permanent or semi-permanent display. The action of placing a model in a case immediately creates a barrier between the model and the viewing audience. Undue reflections of the room lighting and the fact that the viewer cannot get close to the model because of the display case all tend to give the audience only relatively superficial interest.

When the model has served its purpose, then it must be stored for future reference. A rack constructed from timber, with wide chipboard shelves is ideal for this purpose, and the models should of course be sealed in plastic bags before they are placed on the shelves. The location of the rack should be away from direct sunlight, in a room where the temperature does not fluctuate between extremes, and the models should be turned about every few weeks so that if any fading takes place it is spread over all elevations of the model buildings and is therefore not noticeable. If, however, space is not available for a rack to store models, an alternative is for 'mirror hangers' to be attached to the rear of the bases, and the models hung from rails by wire hooks.

It goes without saying that all possible steps should be taken to prevent dust settling on models. There are times however when it is unavoidable and a model is returned to the studio or workshop after a display session of several weeks without a cover. To remove dust a soft artists' brush should be used to lift the dust from most surfaces so that it can be blown away. More persistent dust can be removed with a domestic vacuum cleaner using the 'fishtail' adaptor or alternatively making a wooden bung to fit into the vacuum cleaner nozzle then drilling it out to accept a length of $\frac{1}{4}''$ diameter rubber tubing. The reduction in effective diameter of the cleaner nozzle increases the suction force, and the flexible rubber tubing makes it easier to reach into difficult corners.

24. The trade mark emblem on this office block is made from a piece of toothpaste tube

Acknowledgements

We wish to thank the following firms for their assistance and permission to use their registered trade marks where necessary in the preparation of this book.

Firm	Acknowledged for
Bostik Limited, Leicester, England.	for 'Bostik Clear Adhesive', part of the Bostik series of adhesives and sealants.
Impact Garage Advisory Limited, High Street, Mortlake, London, S.W.14.	for the use of photographs of models of Garages, Petrol Filling Stations, Houses, etc. built by the Impact Group, and for the facilities to photograph the author at work in their Model Making Studio.
Letraset Limited, 17–19 Valentine Place, Webber Street, London, S.E.1.	for Letraset transfer letters and symbols, and Letratone shading patterns.
Modelmaking Materials Supply Company, 12 Maclise Road, London, W.14.	for 'Trafficast' and model making materials generally.
George Rowney & Company Limited, P.O. Box 10, Bracknell, Berkshire.	for 'Cryla' Polymer Acrylic Emulsion paints.
Sellotape Products Limited, 54–58 High Street, Edgware, Middlesex.	for 'Sellotape Clear Tape', which is only one of a large range of Sellotape products.
Stanley Works (Great Britain) Limited, Woodside, Sheffield, England.	for Stanley knives and other hand tools.

We would also like to thank McCutchon Studio Ltd., 29, Milson Rd.,
London W14 0L1
and
John Wallwork Ltd., Manchester, for permission to use their photos.

Fractions of an inch to millimetres conversion chart

$\frac{1}{32}$″	=	0·79 mm	1″	=	25·40 mm
$\frac{1}{16}$″	=	1·58 mm	$1\frac{1}{2}$″	=	38·10 mm
$\frac{3}{32}$″	=	2·37 mm	2″	=	50·80 mm
$\frac{1}{8}$″	=	3·17 mm	3″	=	76·20 mm
$\frac{3}{16}$″	=	4·74 mm	4″	=	101·60 mm
$\frac{1}{4}$″	=	6·35 mm	6″	=	152·40 mm
$\frac{3}{8}$″	=	9·52 mm	12″	=	304·80 mm
$\frac{1}{2}$″	=	12·70 mm	36″	=	914·40 mm

Appendix B(i)

Balsa wood

3″ × 4″	3″ × 3/16″	1/2″ × 3/32″
3″ × 3″	3″ × 1/8″	1/2″ × 1/16″
3″ × 2″	3″ × 3/32″	3/8″ × 3/8″
3″ × 1 1/2″	3″ × 1/16″	3/8″ × 1/4″
3″ × 1″	3″ × 1/32″	3/8″ × 3/16″
2″ × 2″	2″ × 1/2″	3/8″ × 1/8″
2″ × 1 1/2″	2″ × 3/8″	3/8″ × 3/32″
2″ × 1″	2″ × 1/4″	3/8″ × 1/16″
1 1/2″ × 1 1/2″	2″ × 3/16″	1/4″ × 1/4″
1 1/2″ × 1″	2″ × 1/8″	1/4″ × 3/16″
1″ × 1″	2″ × 3/32″	1/4″ × 1/8″
4″ × 1/2″	2″ × 1/16″	1/4″ × 3/32″
4″ × 3/8″	2″ × 1/32″	1/4″ × 1/16″
4″ × 1/4″	1″ × 1/2″	3/16″ × 3/16″
4″ × 3/16″	1″ × 1/4″	3/16″ × 1/8″
4″ × 1/8″	3/4″ × 3/4″	3/16″ × 3/32″
4″ × 3/32″	1/2″ × 1/2″	3/16″ × 1/16″
4″ × 1/16″	1/2″ × 3/8″	1/8″ × 1/8″
4″ × 1/32″	1/2″ × 1/4″	1/8″ × 3/32″
3″ × 1/2″	1/2″ × 3/16″	1/8″ × 1/16″
3″ × 3/8″	1/2″ × 1/8″	3/32″ × 3/32″
3″ × 1/4″		1/16″ × 1/16″

Timber: Lime

Approx. Thickness	Approx. Width
1 1/2″	2″
1 1/2″	3″
1 1/2″	4″
1 1/2″	5″
1 1/2″	6″

Hardwood Strip: Spruce

Section

$\frac{3}{16}'' \times \frac{3}{16}''$	$\frac{1}{4}'' \times \frac{1}{2}''$	$\frac{3}{32}'' \times \frac{3}{32}''$
$\frac{3}{16}'' \times \frac{1}{4}''$	$\frac{3}{8}'' \times \frac{3}{8}''$	$\frac{1}{8}'' \times \frac{1}{8}''$
$\frac{3}{16}'' \times \frac{3}{8}''$	$\frac{1}{2}'' \times \frac{1}{2}''$	$\frac{1}{8}'' \times \frac{3}{16}''$
$\frac{3}{16}'' \times \frac{1}{2}''$	$\frac{1}{16}'' \times \frac{1}{16}''$	$\frac{1}{8}'' \times \frac{1}{4}''$
$\frac{1}{4}'' \times \frac{1}{4}''$	$\frac{1}{16}'' \times \frac{1}{8}''$	$\frac{1}{8}'' \times \frac{3}{8}''$
$\frac{1}{4}'' \times \frac{3}{8}''$	$\frac{1}{16}'' \times \frac{1}{4}''$	$\frac{1}{8}'' \times \frac{1}{2}''$

Dowels: Birch

Diameter

$\frac{1}{8}''$	$\frac{3}{8}''$	$\frac{1}{2}''$
$\frac{3}{16}''$	$\frac{7}{16}''$	$\frac{5}{8}''$
$\frac{1}{4}''$		

Polystyrene sheet

Smooth finish extruded high impact rigid sheet.

Ideal for the construction of model buildings. Simple to cut, join and finish. Can be used in combination with card, timber and Perspex, etc.

Thicknesses up to 0·030″ have **matt** surface on each side. Above 0·030″ in thickness material may have **matt** surface on one side only, or both sides, according to maker's available stock.

Supplied in opaque **white** or **black** in the approximate Sheet Sizes given below.

Thickness	Sheet Size
0·015″ ($\frac{1}{64}$″, 0·37 mm)	54″ × 24″ (139 cm × 60 cm)
	27″ × 24″ (69 cm × 60 cm)
	24″ × 18″ (60 cm × 46 cm)
	18″ × 12″ (46 cm × 30 cm)
	12″ × 9″ (30 cm × 23 cm)
0·020″ ($\frac{1}{50}$″, 0·51 mm)	54″ × 24″ (139 cm × 60 cm)
	27″ × 24″ (69 cm × 60 cm)
	24″ × 18″ (60 cm × 46 cm)
	18″ × 12″ (46 cm × 30 cm)
	12″ × 9″ (30 cm × 23 cm)
0·030″ ($\frac{1}{32}$″, 0·75 mm)	54″ × 24″ (139 cm × 60 cm)
	27″ × 24″ (69 cm × 60 cm)
	24″ × 18″ (60 cm × 46 cm)
	18″ × 12″ (46 cm × 30 cm)
	12″ × 9″ (30 cm × 23 cm)
0·040″ ($\frac{1}{25}$″, 1·02 mm)	54″ × 24″ (139 cm × 60 cm)
	27″ × 24″ (69 cm × 60 cm)
	24″ × 18″ (60 cm × 46 cm)
	18″ × 12″ (46 cm × 30 cm)
	12″ × 9″ (30 cm × 23 cm)

Thickness	Sheet Size
0·060″ ($\frac{1}{16}$″, 1·50 mm)	54″ × 24″ (139 cm × 60 cm)
	27″ × 24″ (69 cm × 60 cm)
	24″ × 18″ (60 cm × 46 cm)
	18″ × 12″ (46 cm × 30 cm)
	12″ × 9″ (30 cm × 23 cm)
0·080″ ($\frac{1}{12}$″, 2·04 mm)	54″ × 24″ (139 cm × 60 cm)
	27″ × 24″ (69 cm × 60 cm)
	24″ × 18″ (60 cm × 46 cm)
	18″ × 12″ (46 cm × 30 cm)
	12″ × 9″ (30 cm × 23 cm)

Clear acrylic sheet. Supplied only in the sheet sizes given below.

Plexiglas

Thickness	Dimensions
$\frac{1}{32}''$ (0·79 mm)	28″ × 20″ (71 × 50 cm)
	20″ × 14″ (50 × 35 cm)
	14″ × 10″ (35 × 25 cm)
	10″ × 7″ (25 × 17 cm)

Perspex

Thickness	Dimensions
$\frac{1}{25}''$ (1·01 mm)	36″ × 24″ (91 × 60 cm)
	24″ × 18″ (60 × 45 cm)
	18″ × 12″ (45 × 30 cm)
	12″ × 9″ (30 × 22 cm)
$\frac{1}{16}''$ (1·58 mm)	36″ × 24″ (91 × 60 cm)
	24″ × 18″ (60 × 45 cm)
	18″ × 12″ (45 × 30 cm)
	12″ × 9″ (30 × 22 cm)
$\frac{3}{32}''$ (2·37 mm)	36″ × 24″ (91 × 60 cm)
	24″ × 18″ (60 × 45 cm)
	18″ × 12″ (45 × 30 cm)
	12″ × 9″ (30 × 22 cm)
$\frac{1}{8}''$ (3·17 mm)	36″ × 24″ (91 × 60 cm)
	24″ × 18″ (60 × 45 cm)
	18″ × 12″ (45 × 30 cm)
	12″ × 9″ (30 × 22 cm)
$\frac{5}{32}''$ (3·95 mm)	36″ × 24″ (91 × 60 cm)
	24″ × 18″ (60 × 45 cm)
	18″ × 12″ (45 × 30 cm)
	12″ × 9″ (30 × 22 cm)
$\frac{3}{16}''$ (4·74 mm)	36″ × 24″ (91 × 60 cm)
	24″ × 18″ (60 × 45 cm)
	18″ × 12″ (45 × 30 cm)
	12″ × 9″ (30 × 22 cm)

Perspex (cont.)

Thickness	Dimensions
$\frac{1}{4}''$ (6·35 mm)	36″ × 24″ (91 × 60 cm)
	24″ × 18″ (60 × 45 cm)
	18″ × 12″ (45 × 30 cm)
	12″ × 9″ (30 × 22 cm)
$\frac{5}{16}''$ (7·93 mm)	36″ × 24″ (91 × 60 cm)
	24″ × 18″ (60 × 45 cm)
	18″ × 12″ (45 × 30 cm)
	12″ × 9″ (30 × 22 cm)
$\frac{3}{8}''$ (9·52 mm)	36″ × 24″ (91 × 60 cm)
	24″ × 18″ (60 × 45 cm)
	18″ × 12″ (45 × 30 cm)
	12″ × 9″ (30 × 22 cm)
$\frac{1}{2}''$ (12·7 mm)	36″ × 24″ (91 × 60 cm)
	24″ × 18″ (60 × 45 cm)
	18″ × 12″ (45 × 30 cm)
	12″ × 9″ (30 × 22 cm)